500*

HAVELOCK ELLIS: Artist of Life

Havelock Ellis:
ARTIST OF LIFE

A Study of His Life and Work

BY

JOHN STEWART COLLIS

WILLIAM SLOANE ASSOCIATES
New York   1959

Preface

There are the artists; there are the martyrs; there are the saints;
there are the prophets; there are the saviours; there are the lib-
erators: and there are those who combine many of these forms
of Heroism: these are the gods, and they do come into the
world from time to time, and pass through it, and the world
does not take much heed of them. But they make their in-
effaceable mark; they remain with us always; they are im-
mortally here, ever ready to heal and to save.

I often call to mind Stephen Spender's splendid line—'I
think continually of those who were truly great.' For many
years I have continually thought of the greatness of Havelock
Ellis. My approach to him was first made at the literary, philosophical, religious end. And that again is my approach here.
'Only a complete mastery of his work can justify breaking the
silence of one's respect for Havelock Ellis,' said Waldo Frank.
A good remark; I subscribe to it. But insofar as his centenary
is now coming round, and since he asked me to write the Introduction to his *Selected Essays* for the Everyman Library
and took a favourable view of my interpretation, I feel I
should try my hand at presenting the man, the life, and the
work—as one person sees them.

I wish to make it clear that while I have presented his work
with some degree of adequacy I do not claim to have written
at the same time a very elaborate biography. I hope I have
brought out what is relevant and significant during the most
creative years of his life, being content to leave the elabora-
tion of exhaustive detail to other hands.

HAVELOCK ELLIS: Artist of Life

1

WHEN about to depart, I said—"What was your ship?"
He took the point and seemed amused. For in his old
age Havelock Ellis did look rather like a sea captain. We do
not see this in the photographs; but that is the impression I
got when I visited him at Herne Hill in 1938. I did not then
know that the prevailing vocation of his forefathers on both
sides was the sea, and that his father was a captain in whose
ship the son, starting at the age of seven, more than once
sailed round the world—literally *sailed*. Though the sea has
played such a large part in the life of England it has played
but a small part in the ancestry of her men of genius. The
complicated and far-spread maritime ancestry of Havelock
Ellis is rare indeed in the English spiritual field. The fluid,
libertarian, adventurous, versatile spirit, which he found in
himself, together with the far sight and the horizoned outlook, were, he felt, the characteristic outcome of the sailor's
life. He was represented on both sides by families of sailors
and people connected with the sea, while farther back, also on
both sides, "is a long line of parish priests, solid, scholarly,
admirable men, tenacious of their convictions, ready to suffer
cheerfully for their devotion to those convictions. In my
blood the two latent streams of tendency have entered into
active combination and grown conscious at last in my brain.

So I have become an adventurer in morals and a pioneer over spiritual seas." [1]

His grandparents possessed the intellectual and artistic temperament, which his parents transmitted to him though they themselves showed no trace of it. His father was a simple, efficient, genial, handsome, superficial, mediocre, and thus extremely happy man. Going to sea early he passed half a century in a sailor's life, becoming the typical English sea-captain, often thought the best kind of man that England produces. He never knew what a headache was like; his teeth remained perfect till old age; indigestion was unknown to him. He was cheerful and sociable, remaining a great favourite of the girls till the end. He never sought to look below the surface of things, while even the manifold surface spectacle of life which he had seen under many aspects in many parts of the world left him untouched. He never discovered beauty, and having neither violent passions to restrain nor exalted aspirations to pacify he had no inner need for religious debate.

It is indeed a priceless gift of fortune for an artist to have a father of that sort. "The Ellises, it may seem," says the son, "have no vices, but they buy that exemption at a price, for one is inclined to ask whether, when the right path is so easy to them, they really have any virtues. Their strength lies in their imperturbable mediocrity." Havelock Ellis always used words with an exactitude which I have long held before me as an ideal, regardless of any debased or stupid meaning they may have acquired. He was fully aware of what he owed to his father. "I owe much to the mediocrity of the Ellises. It is true that so far from being cheerfully content with the surface of things, I am a restless searcher below surfaces," he says. "But yet there has always been that precious modifying influence of the Ellis temperament. The disposition that finds its expression mainly in literary channels is usually tempted to adopt a view of life that is one-sided, excessive, or eccentric.

[1] *My Life.* I propose to quote a number of short passages, and a few longer ones, from the Autobiography. Throughout, anything henceforth in quotation marks, with no reference, is to be taken as from *My Life.*

If I have been able on the whole to maintain a wide and sunny view of life, not merely to escape the greed of wealth and of honour, but to temper the ardour of my faith and enthusiasm by a pervading reasonableness—a scepticism that smiles at all my failures—I think I owe it largely to that temperate and cheerful acceptance of the world which is part of the mediocrity of the Ellises. My life would have been happier had I possessed more of it."

The mothers of remarkable men are invariably remarkable themselves—for good or for evil. H.E.'s mother was no exception. (I will now venture to refer to him throughout as H.E., rather than as Havelock Ellis or as Ellis: I always think of him myself as H.E., and I hope the reader will not find it offensive). She was in no way distinguished intellectually, but possessed great energy and force of character. Never in the least beautiful, her vitality attracted many suitors, and in the end she chose Captain Ellis in the teeth of her father's admonition never to marry a sailor. At the age of seventeen she was converted. Unfortunately this was combined with an adherence to an Evangelical creed demanding the avoidance of "worldliness." Many Victorian women (as if they felt that the Queen had an eye on them) displayed an infinite capacity for not enjoying themselves and promoted the greatest unhappiness of the greatest number around them—which was called Respectability. After her conversion Mrs. Ellis never entered a theatre again, and even when invited by a rich aunt to visit Paris she declined, feeling it wrong to go to so wicked a city. In this way she may seem to resemble the mother of John Ruskin. Yet it was not so. Though she had stopped the flow of her own rich and volatile nature she put no pressure upon others to follow her example. It was a family of five; H.E. was the eldest, the remaining four being girls. There was no question of her spoiling and half-laming her son in the Mrs. Ruskin manner, for she was really a great and good woman in spite of her piety. And there was nothing in the nature of the Victorian domestic interior as symbolized by the Samuel Butler household. The marriage problem was solved by the husband being absent for nine months of the year. The three months which they annually spent together were extremely happy, and their son never witnessed a single conjugal jar or domestic scene, nothing remotely resembling, for instance, the D. H. Lawrence family circle. Both Mrs. Ruskin and Mrs. Lawrence did their best, and half-succeeded, in destroying their sons, and were in no wise checked by their husbands. Mrs. Ellis reigned supreme in the home without friction. Her husband enjoyed as much command as he needed on board his ship. At home "however bravely he might whistle and loudly call for his boots, it was not with the easy assurance of mastership he shouted his orders on deck or damned the steward below"— for he felt that at home his wife was the captain.

We have heard a good deal about the horrors of the Victorian household, and I do not think that there has been exaggeration. We recognise the service that Samuel Butler performed with his famous time-bomb which blew up. The sins of the mothers and the fathers were visited upon the fathers and the mothers, and one of the most pleasing aspects of *The Way Of All Flesh* is the fact that there is absolutely no let-up in Butler's attack upon his mother. It is rare indeed when a gifted son is not at least half-ruined by his mother. It was not so in the Ellis family. Mrs. Ellis could have maimed her son—even H.E. She could have halved him, she could have uncentred him, for the man has not yet been born who in his childhood is a match for his mother if she choose to exert the full force of her will, be it in terms of love, or, as sometimes happens, in terms of hate. H.E. was marvellously lucky in his mother. He who had it in him to be among the whole men, to be a harmonious man, he whose spirit was to pass with compassion across the whole world, was in no way thwarted by his mother. A man's view of women is determined, far more than many of us would admit, by the kind of mother he has had. H.E. admits this. He thought that his father was a little weak, while he knew that his mother was a tower of strength—though never exerted against the unfolding of the son. "Throughout life I have possessed an instinctive and unreasoned faith in women, a natural and easy acceptance of the belief that they are entitled to play a large part in many fields of activity. The spectacle of my mother's great and unconscious power," he adds, "certainly counted for much in that faith and that belief."

2

HAVELOCK ELLIS was born on the second of February, 1859, after a night of raging tempest, in old Croydon. There was nothing tempestuous or abnormal about the baby who was robust, though the child became delicate. His earliest recollections seem to date from the age of two—(which strikes a person like myself as extraordinary who can remember nothing before the age of nine). At four his first sister was born, and on seeing her he is said to have exclaimed, "take away that piece of dirt and rubbish," though it was an uncharacteristic remark, for the baby was soon the object of his care and attention. He claims that there was nothing remarkable or precocious about his childhood, but adds that he easily learnt to read by the age of five. Though not goody-goody he was a "good" child lacking in the impulses of pugnacity and the vices of boyhood that are so often virtues in disguise, and was already nearly as shy, sensitive, and reserved as he was later to become—though by no means wholly so, for he was known to laugh at this age, to get excited by a circus, and to sing in public!

At the age of seven he took his first voyage round the world in his father's ship, the *Empress*, a wooden sailing vessel, and wrote home to his mother saying—"I like travelling though I should not wish to be a sailor," and after expressing admiration for Sydney added, "I was much amused by the trees in the Government Gardens, reading their names and

the countries they came from, some of them with more flowers than leaves, and the others very curious"—sentences which
might have been written at any age. While on this voyage he
mentions how one day he was watching the ship's cat making
his way between the rails at the ship's stern. Its position was
perilous, a touch would send him into the sea. Moved by a
sudden impulse the boy supplied that touch. "I at once went
to my father and told him that the cat had fallen overboard
and a rope was thrown over, but the cat had already disappeared. No one suspected me of any part in the cat's death,
and I never revealed to anyone—I believe unto this day—that
I was guilty in the matter. I have always, however, regarded
it as a criminal act."

When he was about nine the family went to live in a district between Wimbledon and Merton, and there he went to
school. Reading now became his passion, and amongst all
sorts of other books he discovered in the drawers of an old
bureau all the volumes of *Nature Displayed*, a conspectus of
the whole realm of Nature, popular yet with no sacrifice of
scientific honesty and precision. He pored over them with
minute attention. "There are no such books now, for modern
taste supposes that 'popular science' must be made easy and
vague and sentimental and prudish, but for my part, when I
was ten years old much as now when I am sixty years old, I
wanted truth presented to me as it is, arduous and honest and
implacable." At the age of twelve he was carefully reading
Macaulay and Milton and Burns and Longfellow and Scott
and Defoe. Suddenly he got a fever for reading *The Boys of
England*—extravagantly sensational and romantic adventures
in wild and remote lands. The fever subsided as suddenly as it
had arisen, probably only lasting a few weeks, and left not
a trace behind, though while it lasted it was an excitement
which overwhelmed all ordinary considerations. At the same
age he had prepared a little book for publication called "The
Precious Stones of the Bible," accumulating with an open
mind all the information he could acquire, a natural history
method native to him. He decided to publish twelve copies,

but, finding that this would cost twelve pounds, the scheme
was dropped. He planned another book on flowers and wrote
a number of essays on various topics in a sermonizing manner.
There was no stimulus from outside directing him into these
channels, since he had never met an author and people of that
sort were unknown in his family circle. It was pure instinct.

He harboured no sexual emotions or curiosities at this time,
though he did consider the question as to the origin of babies
and decided that they emerged from their mothers' navels, a
purely scientific question involving, he says, no morbid feelings. He was affectionately devoted to his mother, but this
was without touch of excess and without cravings for manifestations of love from her, and without the slightest hostile
feeling towards his father. Nor was there any question of
suppression or repression going on within him. He thought it
superfluous. "This fact now seems to me of immense significance for the whole of my life; it is, from one point of view,
the key to all my work and my whole attitude towards the
world. I have never repressed anything. What others have
driven out of consciousness or pushed into the background, as
being improper or obscene, I have maintained and even held
in honour. It has become wrought into the texture of my
whole work."

Thus already at the age of twelve we have got something
here. And now, at the same advanced age, he was to discover
beauty. As we know, beauty has to be discovered, and we
come upon it just as we come upon gold or coal or oil or
uranium. The most usual way of finding it is by finding something else—a girl for instance. The only daughter of his
mother's step-brother, Agnes, aged sixteen, was invited to stay
with the Ellises on a visit to Wimbledon. Dark, pretty, and
vivacious she treated him with easy familiarity and won his
heart completely. They would walk and play together and she
would sometimes make him offer her his arm and treat her as
a grown-up lady. In due course she returned home. He never
saw her again. He made no effort to do so—which was entirely typical of him. He never wrote. He never mentioned

her name, no one knew that he thought of her. Yet he was
devoured by a boy's pure passion, and with streaming eyes
would pray to God that one day they would be married.

He had seen her beauty; and now, looking round, he observed that the earth was beautiful. He began to revel in Nature, to enjoy art, to write verse. "Love comes normally to a
child through what we call the soul rather than through the
body." Any stray spark from the real world may generate
within the boy a spiritual passion apparently lacking in any
sensual element. "A chance encounter of life sets free within
him a vision which has danced within the brains of his ancestors to remote generations and has no relation whatever to the
careless girl whose playful hand opens the dark casement that
reveals the universe."

3

NOW that he had reached twelve his parents decided to send him to a boarding-school, and he went to the Poplars at Tooting. Both the headmaster and his wife were oddities (nothing unusual in the nineteenth century which produced far more eccentrics than exist today) but the school was commonplace enough and inspired no love of learning, and he continued without aptitude for formal studies, picking up no Greek and so little Latin that he was obliged to acquire it later in life. But there was a good French master, and by means of this man he rapidly learnt the language and with a little help from him out-of-hours learnt German and Italian as well. "My interest in French, and in modern languages generally, simply as instruments to bring me nearer to contemporary life and contemporary literature and contemporary peoples, has been of inestimable value to my work, as well as a perpetual source of delight and of refreshment, and I am grateful to Joseph Stevens, I do not say for implanting but for stimulating and fostering it." Those of us familiar with his work know what these words mean. They mean that in his maturity his mind moved with ease across the European intellectual scene, the French, the German, the Italian, the Spanish, and the Scandinavian, so that we find him interpreting their modern thinkers, playwrights, and poets before they were translated into English.

More important was another master called Angus Mackay,

a Scot of great character, intelligence, and enthusiasm. His real passion was for literature, especially poetry, being familiar with contemporary movements, and the author of some good verse himself. The existence of this man here was a wonderful thing for the shy and eager boy of twelve. Here was a man full of the life and energy of the outer world and inspired by its culture. "I had travelled round the earth, but I had never in my life conversed with a cultured intellectual man." Meeting Mackay was a revelation for little H.E. He had already begun to read widely as we have seen, but now Mackay opened for him the riches of English nineteenth-century literature, manifestations of the human spirit he had never suspected. More than this he *talked with him*. He discussed great questions, striking sharply across the beliefs and conventions which the boy had grown up in without ever thinking them out. In fact he realised for the first time that such Questions existed, that there were great aspirations beyond the personal, great ideals to be passionately fought for. A touch had awakened his soul and intellect which henceforth would work at no man's bidding nor be turned aside by any man's resistance.

Relying upon my instinct for what is significant in my story, I have not hesitated to emphasize the importance of H.E.'s association with Mackay and the French master. For these are the key moments in the winding up of the clock of psychic tension in the lives of those who do things in this world. There are men of destiny and there are men of fate. Those who are men of destiny are inclined to meet the right man at the right moment and come upon the right book at the right time. Perhaps I should put it more simply and say that when we are men of destiny we *use* our man who generally does appear, and when we are men of fate we fail to do so and drift on helplessly through life.

H.E. was unable to employ anyone in this manner at the Poplars in terms of science. This was not ultimately disastrous, but it was an impediment. The boy possessed an extraordinary balance of power. The pressure within him to become a literary artist was not greater than the pressure to be a scientific

investigator or natural historian. But at this school there was
no one who possessed the scientific spirit or who was interested in imparting scientific knowledge, and so he had to obtain, on his own initiative, manuals in natural philosophy,
chemistry, geology, and botany. He met no one there who
had learnt to observe, or who really loved, Nature in her
processes. "If I had personally known someone who could
have shown me how our daily life is full of chemical problems, someone to whom the names, structures and uses of
plants were familiar, someone who would have made me see
the vital mechanism of animals and men, I should probably
have been greatly helped and saved from wasting much time."
We may well believe so! For at the age of twelve he was
already interested in exact measurement and had discovered
that stature varies during the day. It was not till he became a
medical student at St Thomas's Hospital eleven years later that
he began to observe accurately as a matter of course and to
comprehend the scientific temper—and to discover how rare
it is to find that temper even among professional men of
science.

Still, I do not think the school did badly by him. We must
not expect too much. I take the liberty to say, in passing, that
Havelock Ellis did not inspire me to try and bring science
and literature together. The remark about chemistry just
quoted meant nothing to me when I read it first, for while his
interest in science was active at the age of twelve I did not
make that approach until the age of forty. I used to be annoyed with the type of person who says—"I was put off
Shakespeare by the way he was done in school with all those
notes and annotations." For it seemed to me inconceivable
that anyone could be put off Shakespeare or the New Testament by schoolmasters or annotations, since personally I went
straight for the word-music without giving such things a
moment's consideration. But I suppose the weaker brethren
could be led into some sort of appreciation by right methods
—or some of the put-off people could. For I have to remember that I was put off science by the way it was annotated

or introduced: it was just "stinks," or something you did in a laboratory with test-tubes, and I received no clue to the fact that science is poetry in another mode. My instinct being weak in this direction I could have benefited by being led by the hand before leading myself twenty years later. But when thinking of H.E., we are to remember that by the age of twelve he had reached the position which few attain even by the age of forty. He was to become a great artist—which is rarer than being a genius. He was also a genius—in comprehension. And that, in my opinion, is the rarest of all forms of genius.

Though the boy's mental development began to go ahead favourably and swiftly at this period it was also made a hell for some time by one boy. The old story of the bully raises its ugly head and I should not pass it over. This boy liked riding horses and later joined the Indian Frontier Mounted Police. Having no horse at school he conceived the idea of employing H.E. as one. He made spurs out of pins and every night he mounted on H.E.'s back and rode him round and round the room in his nightshirt. This equestrianism was an acute nervous torture, but lacking all instincts of pugnacity, the idea of resisting or of attacking his rider never occurred to H.E. "I performed the required duties much as a real animal would have done, without articulate protest or complaint." This came to an end when his mother, discovering something amiss with him, made him confess what was going on, and arranged with the headmaster to have him placed in another room.

He left school at the age of sixteen and lived at home, acting as tutor to two of his sisters. He did not know what profession he was going to take up. When Diderot, the marvellous encyclopædist, was asked in his youth what he wanted to be he replied—"nothing." Yet for him this meant something like "everything." So with H.E. But he was greatly troubled all the same by his lack of definite vocational aim, knowing that he would never manage to pursue any aim which no passionate instinct drew him towards. His parents were only mildly concerned. "Do not worry about Harry," said his mother to his

father with a confidence that impressed him. It was a long
time before the son realized how right she was. He had no
worldly ambition. He was not filled with the divine desire for
praise—a stimulus evidently unnecessary to him. He never
sought to be in "the public eye." He did not wish to be "a
celebrity." He never envisaged even the smallest bit of lime-
light. He did not want beautiful women to whisper at a cock-
tail party—"that's him." He abhorred the idea of belonging to
the company of what Keats called "the little famous." He
never thought about the business of "winning a position in the
world," until late in life he found that that position was won.
He loved the phrase—"As if the emerald should say, at all
costs I must be emerald." He would be emerald: he would be
himself, whatever happened—that was his sort of rule one.
He would use with honesty and courage the mixed material
put into his hands at the outset, his own nature, and carry out
the work which that nature and Nature—they seemed one to
him—had set him to do. And this he did. It brought dividends.
He was surprised to find at the end of his life how great had
been the response, how rich the reward. It seemed strange and
wonderful to him that for this he should be held in honour:
"it had never entered into my wildest dreams of life; indeed I
have never had dreams of life in which I myself played any
prominent part. I could not understand why what was so
simple and natural and inevitable to me should mean much to
others. But perhaps it is only just that the world which has
brought so many miracles into my life should in the end be
rewarded by finding in me a miracle." The modesty of Havelock Ellis has annoyed some people: his non-modesty has
annoyed others. It is the privilege of the few natural men,
the whole men, who visit this earth from time to time, to
write of themselves as they please, with cool detachment. It
is for those of us who are not whole men, who see life un-
steadily and see it half, to mind our step.

   He knew from the beginning that he possessed a certain
dogged persistence, obstinacy, determination to follow his
own path and work out his own nature, but the immediate

problem was to find if there was some kind of career he could pursue compatible with this. One possible career at this time wavered before him. Many of his ancestors had been parsons. The religious life was in his blood. Should he pursue it? At this period he was accustomed to go about with a little Testament in his pocket, and for years he had been stirred by the preaching of the Rev. Erck, a great Irish orator, who had been vicar at Merton. But can the idea that he would ever preach from a pulpit have seriously entered his head?

In any event this vague notion soon passed because at about this time he began to slide quietly off the foundation of Christian belief. While still at school he had bought Renan's *Life of Jesus*, but he had read it in a critical spirit. Now Swinburne's *Songs Before Sunrise* and Shelley's poems began to exert a more powerful influence. And then an external event sealed his destiny. His father was due to sail to Sydney. Since the boy was not robust and suffered from abdominal pain, it occurred to his parents that another voyage round the world would be just the thing for him before he settled down to earn a living. The decision was made and acted upon without fuss and without any of the parties being aware that the whole life of the boy hinged upon it.

Thus he set out, at the age of sixteen. "My definite memories of the voyage are fused with all my memories of voyages on the sea, with the magic of a sailing ship—so exquisitely responsive to Nature, sometimes idly calm upon a glassy ocean, sometimes swiftly driven onwards, furling and unfurling her canvas wings to the breeze—of the vast blue foam-crested rhythmic waves of the South Atlantic, of the wild free birds of the sea, above all the albatross and the gull." I quote those words because they are all he has to say about his experiences of the sea on board, experiences which for most writers would have been priceless "copy." He seldom used his descriptive power. It was not a lyric power, never rhapsodic, but its flowing exactitude of truth, seemingly effortless, as in the above, and as I will show later again on the sea, makes as much an impact as the lyric or the rhapsody. He does not speak about the ocean much, but all his best work is savoured with that salt. Yet I have always found it difficult to forgive him for the sentence with which he opens his chapter on Whitman in *The New Spirit*—"If we put aside imaginative writers—Hawthorne, Poe, Bret Harte, and Mark Twain—America has produced three men of world-wide significance.[1] For this leaves out Herman Melville—of all people it leaves out Melville mind you!

After reaching Sydney the ship was to proceed to Calcutta. Then it was that a Dr. Hughes told the captain that the Indian climate would be unsuitable for his son. It was arranged that he would be given a post as assistant master at a certain Sydney school. And at this school he was settled without delay.

That brought to an end the first stage of his life. He entered the world—quite alone in the southern hemisphere. He could not then know how important it was, or how his whole fate in life hung upon it. It is not quite true to say that we never know what these moments are till we gaze back with the perspective of time. But we seldom do, and H.E. certainly did not when he took up his post at a private school at Burwood near Sydney, New South Wales.

[1] i.e.—Whitman, Thoreau, and Emerson.

4

HIS career as school-master at Burwood was short, for he was soon found inadequate, and after a month was given notice. The fact is he was quite unable to deal with obstreperous children, and even detested them. Having left this school he took a position as tutor in a private family at a place called Goonerwarrie, where he spent a peaceful year, taking in the beauty of the Australian scene, and ever with a book in hand, and writing the appropriate thin volume of verse in sonnet form. Yet this peaceful time was darkened by his religious difficulties. His early faith which he had taken from his mother had fallen from him, just slipped away. *For it was not his own.* When his awakened self gazed at it, he found that it would not bear inspection. True, he had read Renan in a critical spirit, still being fortified in his boyhood beliefs. Now when he read thinkers who were free, he discovered that he agreed with them—his faith was gone.

This often gives pleasure. There is a feeling of liberation and stimulus, the mind leaping forward unchained. It is not always so. In the case of H.E. the faith went easily but not because he wanted it to go or felt that anything was gained by its departure. Nothing replaced it. "By following what seemed to be the call of truth I had merely entered a blank and empty desert." He was repelled by the cold and dead mechanical world with which he thought he was presented as a substitute for his faith. He brooded over "this alien universe of whirling machinery" in which he seemed to be enmeshed much in the same manner as Carlyle's Teufelsdröckh in *Sartor Resartus*, when plunged into the melancholy pit of the Everlasting Nay declared that: "To me the Universe was all void of Life, of Purpose, of Volition, even of Hostility: it was one huge, dead, immeasurable Steam engine, rolling on, in its dead indifference, to grind me limb from limb." The combination of the industrial revolution and the advent of Darwinism contrived to have this effect near the close of the nineteenth century upon many religious minds.

In the meanwhile H.E. resolved to become an assistant master again and obtained a post at a place called Crafton. The headmaster was a young man, pale, thin, and austere with the strained mouth of one who is over-repressing his strong natural instincts in the name of Christianity. In fact the tension was stronger than he could bear, his brain gave way and he was dead the next fortnight, just before the new term was to open. It was proposed that H.E. should succeed him as headmaster. This was a wonderful opening. It was what is known as a Golden Opportunity. It was clear that he could make his fortune at the outset of his career—as indeed his successor had no difficulty in doing. But H.E. was not born for this purpose, and could not seize the opportunity and "go where the lolly is" as Tom, Dick, and Harry would now put it, and do it. "It is useless for Opportunity to present even the most attractive forelock to one who was not born to seize it," he says. "And I was so clearly not born to be a successful headmaster that I have never for a moment regretted my failure to grasp firmly that particular forelock." It was ever so with him. When I first read his Autobiography in 1940 I remembered afterwards, perhaps more clearly than any other remark he made in the book, a passage which ended with the words—"I am a child of Nature, but she has to be a careful artist in what she seeks to make of me, for there are so many things I cannot do." Those final words seemed to me a typical H.E.-ism, and stuck with me—no doubt for subjective reasons also. On rereading the passage it amuses me to note that the exact words are—"I am a child of Nature, but she has to be a careful artist in what she seeks to make of me, there are so many ends I am unfit for."

At the end of nine months the school began to show such clear signs of dwindling away that he decided to sell up and clear out. He accomplished this, it appears, with the maximum of inefficiency. Returning to Sydney he thought it best to qualify as a teacher under the Council of Education which controlled elementary education in New South Wales, and then be in a position to command a teaching job at any time, without the onus of organizing responsibility. A few months later he qualified and received an appointment as teacher in a school at Sparkes Creek, and proceeded thither at once, now at the age of eighteen.

He had been told that it would be easy to find a lodging in the farm-house of an old settler named Ashford at the Creek. It turned out that the old man had no room for him, or pretended that he had none, and after accommodating him for two nights then told him that he must go and live in the schoolhouse. "So I put on my tall silk hat and took up my little bag," he relates, "and went my lonely way to the schoolhouse. I felt very forlorn. Now at last I was completely adrift, altogether, it seemed, cut off from civilisation. I felt like a lost child, and my eyes, as I walked, smarted painfully with unshed tears." He hastens to add that there was no need for tears and that as a matter of fact he never shed them, and that, had he known the good fortune that was attending him at this moment, he might well have seen in imagination such a railing of gold round the schoolhouse he was approaching, as Rousseau desired to erect round the spot at Annecy where he first met Madame de Warens. He met no woman there, and no man, who meant anything to him. The person he found was himself. This was the year 1878—the decisive year of his life.

The situation of his residence was idyllic for him. The house was built about a hundred yards above the creek which was sometimes in a torrent. It consisted of two rooms with separate doors onto a veranda, one for the schoolroom, the other for the teacher. The latter contained nothing but a makeshift bed, its framework consisting of four poles supporting two sacks attached to four legs so imperfectly that the structure would occasionally collapse during the night. There was no more furniture in the room except a little bench to support a tin washing bowl the water for which he obtained from a well nearby. Apart from the addition of some cooking tools,[1] he did not seek to add to the appointments of this establishment, and lacking every kind of gadgetry and impedimenta necessary to a high standard of life, he was free to attend to the furniture of his mind. Those whom the gods love do not always die young: they are sometimes cast in desolate places, such as the Australian bush, to sink or to swim—and for such Favourites the issue is not in doubt.

Having established his material basis he found his professional duties easy to control, requiring little effort or thought, the elementary instruction and routine being laid down by the Council of Education, while these children gave him no trouble. It was his duty to teach not only at Sparkes Creek but also at Junction Creek and this meant a walk over the hills several times a week. For the first time in his life he was really alone with Nature. Moreover, the fauna was new and strange, including cockatoos and parakeets, a few snakes, lizards that lay motionless along the branches of trees, bears who moved away at their leisure on his appearance, and, above all, the graceful bounding kangaroos descending the slopes. He had all this to himself, for on the wonderful walk which he took two days of the week to Junction Creek he passed no human dwelling and met no human being. For the first time in his life he could stand by the cottage door in the evening in the perfect peace of that solitude which is not loneliness—the dream of so many!—and absorb the inexpressible promise; and he could sit by his table in the schoolroom on stormy evenings all his nerves "stirred by the prolonged rhythmic curves of gathered-up winds that rolled and tumbled and

[1] For a list of what he bought see *Kanga Creek: an Australian Idyll*.

crashed through the trees among the hills like an ocean let loose." And once on his return as he approached his hut and saw the roses on the veranda posts against the dark wood, a thrill of rapture, he says, ran through him and he saw roses as he had never seen them before, as he would never see them again.

Now he could expand. Now he could grow. The recluse is not the man who turns his back on mankind and serves only himself; it is more likely that he will seek to find how he may serve mankind. Many years later H.E. wrote in Volume I of *Impressions and Comments:*

It is an error to suppose that Solitude leads away from Humanity. On the contrary it is Nature who brings us near to Man, her spoilt and darling child. The enemies of their fellows are bred, not in deserts, but in cities, where human creatures fester together in heaps. The lovers of their fellows come out of solitude, like those hermits of the Thebaid, who fled far from cities, who crucified the flesh, who seemed to hang to the world by no more than a thread, and yet were infinite in their compassion, and thought no sacrifice too great for a Human Being. . . .

It is known to many that we need Solitude to find ourselves. Perhaps it is not so well known that we need Solitude to find our fellows. Even the Saviour is described as reaching Mankind through the Wilderness.

We might go further. When a man is alone with his self it is really only then that he has a chance of becoming one with the not-self. And so it was with H.E. as we shall presently find.

5

HE WAS now approaching the age of nineteen. Physical and emotional desires were of course acute, but his desire for knowledge was more massive and ever present—and it could be gratified. He gratified it to the utmost. Though in the Australian bush he was able to get books—he does not explain how he managed this—and he got them of all kinds, in English, French, German, and Latin. It is noteworthy that at this time science occupied only a very small place in these studies. I have little doubt that he instinctively, if not consciously, realized that he must *see the whole before he came to the part*. It is unwise to underestimate the importance of this. Those who are forced by their schooling to knuckle down to the particular, the part; those who are made into "science students" at a tender age, have very little chance of ever being able to see the whole. It is perfectly easy, and natural in my opinion, to proceed from synthesis to analysis with excitement and joy, every new revelation of the part enriching one's vision of the whole; but it is not usual for anyone to pass from analysis to synthesis, for he has got so stuck in the part that his imagination has failed to move and he is unable ever to attain a vision of the whole. And it is indeed noteworthy that H.E., though a man who possessed from an early age a genius for both analysis and synthesis, sought first to grasp the whole and avoided becoming bogged in the parts.

Though he got every book he wanted, he selected them carefully and deliberately, avoiding, as always, promiscuous reading, which is the absolute enemy of knowledge and a good deal more harmful than promiscuous love-making. His mind was ranging freely but with discipline, and with the power to grasp what it seized. "I had acquired the power of seeing the world freshly, and seeing it directly, with my own eyes, not through the dulling and disturbing medium of tradition and convention." We need not doubt the truth of this, though he is referring to a youth of nineteen! For we have only to turn to his works to be astonished by the originality of his stance and the acuteness of his angle.

And now he was ready for the most important moment in his life. The hour had come when the religious discord which had distressed him ever since the loss of his boyhood's faith, was to be dissolved in harmony.

Again, what exactly was that discord? There was the clash in his heart and mind between what seemed the discrepancy of two conceptions of the universe. There was the divine vision of life and beauty which he had lost with the perishing of his early religious faith. Over against this there was the scientific conception of an evolutionary world, marvellous in its mechanism but alien to the soul. That, I think, is a fair statement of the famous dichotomy which has strangled many an earnest modern man. When Shaw raged against Darwin for having "banished mind from universe" he was bearing witness to this conflict—and he made it right for himself by shoving the word Creative in front of the word evolution. Still, it occurs to me to wonder whether some readers, who are not over-intellectualized, may feel inclined to ask why the evolutionary mechanism should be alien to the soul.

During these eager reading days at Sparkes Creek H.E. came upon a book called *Life in Nature* by James Hinton. He read it twice. The first time the book made no particular impact, but when by chance he took it up a second time he suddenly became conscious of a personal *revelation*. He saw that the two supposedly conflicting attitudes are really quite harmonious—merely different aspects of the same unity. The Argument of Hinton's book can be stated with brevity. He certainly did see Nature as a mechanism quite as much as any of the mechanists. And he was certainly no Vitalist. A vitalist is a man who makes a hard and fast distinction between Nature and Life. On the one hand there is *dead matter*, and on the other *life* which is somehow in a separate compartment: on the one hand the inorganic and on the other the organic. This was not Hinton's view. He held that organic life was not something new in Nature entangled with the inorganic. He held that there is *nothing more* in the organic than in the inorganic: *all Nature* is living. If we imagine that matter is dead, he argued, our vision is false. The world which had seemed a material world might just as well be seen as a spiritual world. He saw the whole of Nature as one conscious Being. Though he wrote his book with exemplary scientific exactitude his vision lifted him up in spirit and he felt that he could "rest upon the heart and clasp the very living soul of God" and could see that the Earth is infinitely better than any Heaven we can think of. "The Universe is a scene of absolute life and beauty and good; nothing is there that is not so."

Reducing the Argument to simpler terms we may put it this way: there was the doctrine of *materialism* which depressed many people in the nineteenth century. A "materialistic conception" of the universe seemed to deprive it of its glory, to take away its *spiritual* value—for matter was "low" while spirit was "high." In the hands of Hinton this situation was transformed. "You are faced," he said in effect to the depressed victim of "materialistic" science, "by a small ingot you believe to be gold [Life] and a large mass you believe to be clay, and you are told that they are both of the same nature. You jump to the conclusion that they are both clay. *But what I can prove to you is that they are both gold.*" All Nature is alive, he declared, and what we select as life is only "the bright blossom wherein Nature's hidden force comes forth to display itself, the necessary outpouring of the univer-

sal life that circulates within her veins unseen." It is the stream
that has run underground now sparkling in the sun.

This was the Argument of *Life in Nature*, a vitalism a good
deal more satisfactory than the theory of the vitalists who
regard life as a little enclosed cyst in the world, impenetrable
to the laws of Nature. It was presented, says H.E., so clearly
and simply and persuasively and tactfully, and at the same
time with a passionate reverence for nature to which his own
temperament responded, that he was convinced immediately
and completely without effort or struggle. "I had reached the
point at which it sufficed for the situation to be presented to
me in a beautiful and adequate form, and my response could
only be at once that it must be so. In an instant, as it seemed,
the universe was changed for me. I trod on air; I moved in
light." That is his description of the experience in the Autobiography. He referred to it again on three other occasions:
in his Introduction to an edition of *Life in Nature* published in
1932, in an essay called "My Credo" used as a Foreword to
The Genius of Europe published posthumously, and in the
chapter on "The Art of Religion" in *The Dance of Life*.[1] All
the accounts say the same thing, though not in quite the same
words as he never referred back to see how he had previously
put it. His description in *The Dance of Life* is the best known.
He tells how the mechanism of life was no longer viewed as
the mechanism of a factory; it had become vital with warmth
and beauty, it was something that both his intellect and his
heart could gladly embrace. The conception acted upon him
"with the swiftness of an electric contact; the dull aching
tension was removed; the two opposing psychic tendencies
were fused in delicious harmony, and my whole attitude towards the universe was changed. It was no longer an attitude
of hostility and dread, but of confidence and love. My self
was one with the Not-self, my will one with the universal

---

[1] Also, though impersonally, in his essay on Huysmans in *Affirmations* when
speaking of *En Route*, he says the same thing again in ten beautiful lines.
Also in the little, unpublished Diary written between sixteen and twenty.

will. I seemed to walk in light; my feet scarcely touched the ground; I had entered a new world."

I am anxious not to be prolix at this point, but it would be just as wrong to be too brief or to assume that this absolutely fundamental matter, this rock-bottom business, is easily understood. It is easily misunderstood. We have here two distinct things, and we must not think of them as the same thing. We have an Argument and we have an Experience. I have paid due attention to the argument, the reasoning of Hinton's book, though rather against my will—(especially as I once wrote a book called *Farewell to Argument*). The reasoning of the book was merely the instrument which brought about an experience of harmony in H.E. It has probably never done the same for anyone else, and no reader will get hold of a copy with the expectation that it will act upon him in a similar way. It is certainly a brilliant book, and it is marvellously prophetic of our day when "materialism" has undergone such a transformation at the hands of the physicists that now it is child's play to make a delightful intellectual synthesis regarding Mind-and-Matter. But intellectual synthesis is one thing and experience of synthesis—felt as harmony—is another. For H.E. the book was the instrument which happened to make it possible for him to jump from discord to concord. In *The Dance of Life* he says, "I knew that the book was merely the surgeon's touch, that the change had its source in me and not in the book. I never looked into the book again; I cannot tell where or how my copy of it disappeared; for all I know, having accomplished its mission, it was drawn up again to Heaven in a sheet."

The fact is he had experienced a thorough-going religious conversion. It may seem a strange sort to some; but that is because it was particularly pure, because it was particularly free from irrelevant excrescences. The word conversion, of course, has been monstrously misunderstood and distorted and abused by doctrinaires, moralists, clergymen, theologians, and other enemies of religion. It is so often employed to denote someone who has suddenly embraced a new religion. The converted person is conceived as grasping a new and rigid creed, of perhaps changing his whole manner of life, and even of being convicted of sin. This may be the popular idea of conversion, but it is not conversion in its pure form, in its true meaning. It has nothing to do with creeds, it is simply, as the word indicates, a turning round, a complete psychic change, however produced. So far from it necessarily being accompanied by any conviction of sin, it should be accompanied by a conviction of righteousness. This was certainly so in the case of H.E. The two psychic spheres, the intellectual and the emotional, which had been divorced and in constant friction were suddenly united in harmony—and he saw the world not as Ugliness but as Beauty. He had not gained a single new belief that could be expressed in a scientific formula or hardened into a religious creed. The usual questions were not solved: they were dissolved. He was no longer troubled about the "soul" or its destiny, ready to accept any good working analysis of soul which might commend itself. He was no longer troubled about the existence or non-existence of a Supreme Being or Beings, for he was now ready at last to discern that "all the words and forms by which men try to picture spiritual realities are mere metaphors and images of an inward experience. There was not a single clause in my religious creed because I held no creed. I had found that dogmas were—not as I had once imagined true, not as I had afterwards supposed false—but the mere empty shadows of intimate personal experience. I had become indifferent to shadows for I had the substance." In other words he had left behind the hopeless world of intellectual speculation and theory and talk about religion (called theology) and had had religious *experience*. This is the goal and hope of every religious man, of every sage and thinker, for when he has attained it he feels, at long last, *at home in the universe*. And now, instead of using the word *conversion*, or the term *religious experience*, I am free to come to the term I have been waiting to employ— *mystic experience*.

For that is the proper description. Unfortunately it also has become a casualty. It is confused with mystification, though a mystic is a man who is no longer mystified. It is confused with occultism, though it is not a cult of any kind. But however much it has been abused and however much my using it here may put off certain readers whom I would wish to keep by my side, I must not avoid it. For the Mystic Experience, sometimes called Enlightenment, sometimes called Cosmic Consciousness, sometimes called the Perennial Philosophy, though it is an experience which we cannot will, though it is something which cannot be handed from one person having it to another person not having it, is what every religious-minded person wants above all else. But far too many of those people who seem to have been meant for religion are denied that moment of harmony and union, and are forced to promote creeds and moralities as a substitute—the grandest example and the most supreme warning of such, being, perhaps, Tolstoy.

The point to be grasped is that a mystic is a man who has attained a higher stage of consciousness than the normal—even if he only remains in it for a few minutes. As we know, there are really three main stages of consciousness. There is the absolutely primitive stage when there is very little *separation* between Man and Nature—so little that a man could easily think that he was a red parrot. Then there is the tremendously intellectualised state of mind when separation is keenly felt. The very word sin originally meant separation, and the hope was always for atonement—that is at-one-ment again. This is achieved by the mystic on a much more satisfactory plane than previously, since his conscious mind is also at work. He experiences real harmony and consciously calls it harmony, actually declaring that while the experience lasted his self was at one with the Not-self.

I am speaking of mysticism in its purest form. There are many forms and varieties, some quiet, some blinding in their intensity and exaltation, some rationalised instantaneously into theological terms. In the whole of one's reading life I wonder if there is any book so epoch-marking as William James's

Varieties of Religious Experience. When we close it we feel in no doubt as to the genuineness of this glorious cosmic consciousness, this perennial source of happiness and harmony and energy, this dateless and undating data. But the mystic is by no means always the best friend of mysticism. He has been saved. Now he must save others. He rationalizes his experience into a creed and calls upon others, not to attain the experience which he cannot give them, but to believe the creed which he can give them. He is overcome with excitement and exultation. He must cast abroad his news. He must preach. He must spread morality. He must clear the stables and cleanse the city, crying through the streets—with George Fox, the supreme symbol in this kind—"Woe to the bloody city of Lichfield!" His intense conviction draws many followers clinging parasitically to his faulty beliefs while sharing not at all in his divine rapture.

Havelock Ellis was always original—I would say: aboriginal. Few people ever have this experience before the age of thirty-four. He had it at nineteen. And he remained silent. He was filled with joy but he uttered no word about it for forty years. At last he felt constrained to do so in *The Dance of Life*, though it was against his inclination. "To set forth a personal religious experience for the first time requires considerable resolution," he wrote. "Even the fact that more than forty years have passed since the experience took place, scarcely suffices to make the confession of it easy." Nothing could be more characteristic of H.E. or less characteristic of other mystics. He was afraid of killing the experience for himself by talking about it: and that is a danger.

I do not propose to say much more about this now. I could not have said less. He had found his centre. It is the clue to the harmony of his work, his whole *oeuvre*. I have said that he eventually wrote about this four times directly. He also wrote about it once more, though indirectly. I will quote it here. It may serve to answer a question which the reader may well wish to ask. Admitted that this kind of experience cannot be willed, that the Kingdom of Heaven cannot be taken by storm, is there no road that might lead to it? I quote from *Impressions and Comments* Second Series:

Yesterday, here in London, the sky was dark. The rain dropped continuously, one's spirit was dismal. Today the air has been washed clean, the sky is bright, the trees burst into fresh green. Here, as I sit in the Old Garden, the flowers flash with warm radiance beneath the sun, and I hear the deepest wisdom of the world slowly, quietly, melodiously voiced in the throat of the blackbird. I understand. I see the World as Beauty.

To see the World as Beauty is the whole End of Living. I cannot say it is the aim of living. Because the greatest ends are never the result of aiming; they are infinite and our aims can be only finite. We can never go beyond the duty of Saul, the son of Kish, who went forth to seek his father's asses and found a Kingdom. It is only so that the Kingdom of Beauty is won. There is that element of truth in the contention of Bergson, no intellectual striving will bring us to the heart of things, we can only lay ourselves open to the influences of the world, and the living intuition will be born in its own due time.

Beauty is the end of living, not Truth. When I was a youth, by painful struggle, by deliberate courage, by intellectual effort, I won my way to what seemed to be Truth. It was not the end of living. It brought me no joy. Rather, it brought despair; the universe seemed empty and ugly. Yet in seeking the Asses of Truth I had been following the right road.

One day, by no conscious effort of my own, by some inspiration from without, by some expiration from within, I saw that empty and ugly Universe as Beauty, and was joined to it in an embrace of the spirit. The joy of that Beauty has been with me ever since and will remain with me till I die. All my life has been the successive quiet realizations in the small things of the world of that primary realization in the greatest thing of the world. I know that no striving can help us to attain it, but, in so far as we attain, the end of living is reached and the cup of joy runs over.

So I know at such a moment as this, today, as I sit here, alone, in the warm sunshine, while the flowers flame into colour and the birds gurgle their lazy broken message of wisdom, however my life may be shadowed by care, and my heart laden with memories, the essential problems are solved.

It happened that when I first read the *Impressions*, (introduced to the work of H.E. by my friend Bernard Glemser) it was at a period of development when I could do so with full profit. I read with inexpressible thankfulness the words— "we can only lay ourselves open to the influences of the world, and the living intuition will be born in its own due time." For there is a whole philosophy of action towards the attainment of Vision in those words—action not beyond the capacity of anyone to take up. After many years of intellectual "worrying-out" I had adopted the more flexible attitude of passivity and receptivity. This did get me somewhere. My level of mysticism is such a humble one that I do not know if I have any right to use the word. Yet on my own low level the parable of Saul the son of Kish is exactly applicable, for while searching for truth I was so often arrested by beauty that I came to understand at last that the only answer to the riddle of the world is to be able to see the world. And when I came upon the phrase "I see the World as Beauty" I could comprehend its meaning though my own experience went no further than occasional rhapsody. This is something which grows if we allow it to do so by opening ourselves instead of shutting our doors of perception by too much thinking. It may seem to those who would like to have an elaborate scheme of "exercises" and yoga-like practices for the attainment of Vision that the phrase, "we can only lay ourselves open to the influences of the world, and the living intuition will be born in its own due time," gives very little to go on, almost nothing. Well, it was not intended as an exhortation, it was just said in passing; but for those fit to take it up, as we might gather any good thing that falls to the ground, it may turn out to go a long way, to be almost everything.

6

IT IS a commonplace that many girls at the age of seventeen might well be twenty-seven in emotional maturity, while quite a few boys of seventeen might well be seven. It is fair to say that H.E. who was to have more to say about Man and Woman and Sex than most men, was one of these slow developers. He was the kind of young man who is infuriating to the young girl. There were a number of young women emigrating to Australia on his father's ship when he took that last journey; and when he was about to sail the Mate said to the Captain that "young Harry" would be causing havoc among the girls. But the young man never noticed the girls—and would not have done so even if they had been "les girls." His gaze was fixed upon Woman.

There have always been plenty of young men like that. They conceive an Ideal of Glorious Womanhood but pay very little attention to the nice girl within reach. They hardly know what it is to flirt. They are easily put off. On a certain occasion an acquaintance of H.E.'s at Sydney having spent a few hours with his arm round a girl, later on handed her over to him. They walked up and down for a little and then she said—"Ain't the moon lovely?" This was too much for the humourless H.E. at the age of seventeen, and so he fled.

He did not avoid all girls. But he hardly approached them. Sometimes he would adore in silence. While taking his educational course at a place called Grafton he lived amidst a large family named the Chapmans, consisting mostly of girls. He adored May, aged twenty. But he made no advances. He stood afar off, lamenting her fascination. He wrote some verses to her containing a sentiment—Goethe's *"Wenn ich dich liebe, was geht's dich an?"*—which was far too exalted for the occasion, while at the same time he failed to observe that Berta, the sweet undisdainful Berta, did love him, becoming aware of it only when she cried on his departure.

All this is pretty normal for highly intellectual young men. Perhaps they should always be avoided by young women. For they have very little time for sex: they are in a ferment of ideas and ideals. It is not easy for them: they have to grapple with the pressures of sex and of ideas and passion for knowledge all at the same time; they cannot go straight to the goal the girl has in mind for them, and so they prove excessively trying if not impossible. And the irony of it is that the girl, though she herself seldom feels these two pressures and can afford to be single-minded in her aim, actually wants him to have ideals and intellectual interests, even if she has not much strength left for these productions of mankind since she is engaged so much in producing mankind.

It was exceedingly difficult for any girl to have a good time with the young H.E. While he was doing his training for the Educational Certificate, he was friendly with a French Canadian family. The daughter was vivacious, intelligent, uninhibited, and unabashed. He liked her: for French girls were always a good hand at breaking down his reserve, and in the end the happiest days of his life were spent with Françoise Delisle. Yet, as a typical example of his behaviour, once the former made frantic and futile attempts to attract his attention from the opposite side of a theatre. He was in too much of a "brown study" to notice it—characteristic then and at all times. She was a wonderful companion to him. But he never put out his hand in response. When he left he saw her no more. He wrote her no letters. He did not regret her absence, being too absorbed in his ideas and ideals. This passivity, this resistancy to any influence not seeming imperative

to his need, marked him throughout life, especially early in
life, when he would curl up closely against any force which
might mould him the wrong way—whether that force came
from a person or a job. And what was that basic need? It
was to do his work. "Greater love hath no man than this,"
said Gordon Craig, "than that he lay down his life—*for his
work.*" H.E. would not have said that. Yet it was true.

At this time he more or less disdained the women who
were within his reach, while there was yet fermenting within
him an immense thirst for fulfillment—if not now, eventually
—through Woman. And he found that the whole sex problem in the civilization into which he had been born in the
nineteenth century sorely needed airing and cleansing. When
writing about his experiences during his inglorious career at
Burwood he tells how he was invited to the house of a Captain
Fox and enjoyed the company of his pretty and charming
daughters. He says that:

Without being in love with any one of them I vaguely desired
more, yet felt myself powerless, in my inexperienced awkward-
ness, to attain more. All the obscure mysteries of sex stirred
dimly and massively within me; I felt myself groping helplessly
among the difficulties of life. The first faint germ was formed
within me of a wish to penetrate those mysteries and enlighten
these difficulties, so that to those who came after me they might
be easier than they had been to me. The personal situation was,
I suppose, that of nearly every shy and sensitive youth before
my time. But—as I look back half a century later—I see that here
had come a youth whose impulse it was to intellectualise and
moralise his own personal situation, thereby transferring it into
an impersonal form, and universalising it.

In the year 1878, as we have seen, he had solved for himself the religious problem. I have noted how he was silent
about his momentous experience, refraining from publishing
it abroad. He did not set up as a mystic with a message of
salvation. This was not because he failed to consider that the
religious problem was in need of statesmanship; nor did he

feel himself inadequate to deal with it, since after his experience "the whole religious life of the world, the most
extravagant utterances of the most ecstatic mystics, became
simple and natural to me in the light of what I now knew in
the only way in which anything could certainly be known."
He could have done this impersonally. But he did not do so
because he felt that the question of sex came before the question of religion in matter of urgency. It will be best, he
said to himself, to deal with the sex problem first and the
religious problem later. And, as we know, that is what he did.
It took him some thirty years to carry out the first—and no
one knew that it was a mystic who had come to perform
this task! For a person like myself who reached his work
from the other end, reading exclusively his non-scientific
works, it at first seemed extraordinary that such a man, such
an artist, could conceivably concede so much time to an un-
literary enterprise of enormous proportions. But I failed to
realize then that the *Studies* themselves form a work of art,
and that in any case H.E.'s genius for investigation was
every bit as much a part of him as any other aspect. Nor
could I understand then how such a man as I imagined him
to be could possibly have chosen Criminology as the subject
for his first book! That really distressed me, and I have only
now, as a matter of duty, just read *The Criminal*—with
actual enjoyment. The fact is men like H.E. do not pass
through the world very often, and one-siders can hardly be
expected to take him in.

Having determined upon which problem to tackle first in
1878, there now remained the immediate and pressing problem of his practical life. How was he to make a living while
he carried out his vocation? It was a puzzling and painful
problem not easily admitting of a solution. Then suddenly
it became clear. Curiously enough it was again Hinton who
helped him. He had been reading, in a relaxed mood, Hinton's
Letters, and had come upon that part in the narrative when
it had been suggested to the young James that he should enter
the medical profession. H.E. had been reading the book, ly-

ing down on the schoolroom bench. On coming to this point he leapt to his feet as if he had been shot at. "I will become a doctor!" he heard himself exclaim. The question was instantly settled—the question that had worried him so much. Such an idea had never before entered his head. He had always been, and continued to be, extremely bad at making decisions, but he made this one in an instant—and stuck to it. He saw that it was right, not because he ever visualized himself as a practising doctor (which in the event only lasted a short time after he was at last qualified) but because he realized that he needed a doctor's training and to be properly aware of the established conventions of medical science before he could reach his own conception of sex. And again, in the event, this proved an essential step in his mission, for had he not become an accredited practitioner in medicine, surgery, and midwifery, he could never, he declares, have gained a confident grasp of the problems of sex, never set forth his own personal investigations, and never found a decent firm to publish the *Studies*. It would have been a helpless, hopeless struggle, he would have worked in vain and made no mark, all would have been lost; but by adopting the medical profession he acquired the only foundation upon which he could build his work. His choice was inspired, and this engine could now proceed upon its track.

It happened that about this time his parents began to consider the question of his returning to England. This was exactly what he now wanted. His father made arrangements with the captain of a ship returning from Australia to bring him back, and so he came. But though he now knew that he must become an accredited doctor he had not the least idea how the further question was to be solved, as to how he could carry out his medical course, since this would be beyond the resources of his parents. Yet he did not trouble about this. "Perhaps my new faith in the world extended unconsciously even to this practical point. If so, it was to be justified in the most incalculable way. It is, maybe, a simple and instinctive faith in miracles that effects miracles; and my life was full of them."

His sojourn at Sparkes Creek had lasted almost exactly a year—about as long and as fruitful as Thoreau's sojourn at Walden when he "drove Nature into a corner." H.E. said farewell to this spot where so much had been revealed to him. The schoolmaster, Mr. Roberts, shook his hand, commending him for his "pluck at spending twelve months in such an awful hole as Sparkes Creek," while the clergyman, Mr. Shaw, marvelled at his "courage and tenacity," and Mr. Johnson, the inspector, declared that the young fellow should never have been sent to such a place. "How little they all knew," says H.E. looking back, "of the gateways to Heaven!"

7

HE HAD been absent from home for four years, and returned to find his sisters grown-up girls; strangers and yet his sisters, a delightful kind of intimacy he felt. One of them, Laura, who is considered to be most like him, and who was with him at the end, is still with us—at the age of ninety-one, and going strong. Their home was now in a suburb of London near the Crystal Palace. But the question of how to raise money for his medical training was not solved, though his mother could raise £100 for it. In the meanwhile he took up teaching again, and went as assistant master to a school in Birmingham where he experienced for the first time a woman approaching him for sympathy and understanding, and perhaps something else. It was the headmaster's wife, coming to confide, too vaguely, her married troubles; but being hopelessly shy and awkward and inexperienced, he failed her completely.

However, in a short time James Hinton once again helped him! Though somewhat critical of Hinton's writings, in spite of the great service *Life in Nature* had performed for him, he had kept up a general interest in his work, and was now to meet the Hinton family. Hinton had left behind a number of unpublished MSS., and it was the hope of the family that H.E. might do something to aid their publication—a task carried out in the end. Meanwhile the Hintons took an interest in H.E.'s affairs, knowing that he wished to become a doctor, and it was through Howard Hinton that Miss Caroline Haddon, Mrs. Hinton's sister, suddenly offered to lend him £200 for his medical training. Should he accept it? he wondered. Would he ever be able to repay it? He consulted Mackay, his old schoolmaster friend, who emphatically advised him to do so. He did: and his whole life-course was set in motion. "It happened thus, as it had happened before, as it has happened since, throughout my whole life, that, at the right moment, the gift of Heaven, without any effort of mine, fell miraculously upon me. I suppose it is so also for others. And that is why we speak of Heaven and miracles. That is why we try to account for the unaccountable by picturing a fairy-tale God in the skies, who watches over his children and gives them all that they need."

He left Birmingham and came to free board and lodging at home and took up his medical training at St. Thomas's Hospital—a hospital not away in the suburbs but on the banks of the Thames opposite the Houses of Parliament. This was a good spot which he saw under every aspect of day and night for seven years, sometimes catching sight of the political personages of the day: Gladstone "walking along Whitehall, vigorous, alert, well-set, even in old age," or Parnell, "a tall slender man with curiously shifty, self-conscious, timid eyes," or King Edward crossing the bridge in his carriage, playing the game conscientiously in looking "every inch a king," by sitting up stiffly in a manner proper to Royalty and absurd for anyone else.

Here he passed seven years of the medical training and medical examinations. It is well known what a stiff thing this is in itself, and H.E. aimed earnestly at the highest qualifications, while finding much of it, as others do, a desperate drudgery and anxiety, and a lot of the temporary memorizing a fruitless waste of time. Yet during this period he also launched out into many other studies to satisfy the expanding activities of his mind in the field of literature, painting, music, architecture, archaeology, sculpture, philosophy, history, ethics, ethnology, mythology, anthropology, geology, botany,

and physics. Looking back he himself failed to understand
how he managed to squeeze in his medical studies as well,
since these voluntary interests were imperative to his nature
and he had no intention of curtailing them. The immense
range of his knowledge was built up in these years between
1881 and 1889. This fact can be stated: but I have never
been able to understand how it was done, and we will be
obliged to return to this mystery again at the proper place.

The problem is not made any easier by the fact that he
began to write and even to publish at this time, his first considerable effort being an essay on Thomas Hardy; and since
for H.E. it was already a matter of course to investigate a
man's environment before writing about him, he visited Dor-
set and soaked himself in the "Hardy country," and at length
—after spending some days if not weeks over the opening
sentence—came out with an essay which brought a letter
from Hardy himself saying, "I consider the essay a remarkable paper in many ways, and can truly say that the writing
itself, with its charm of style and variety of allusion, occupied my mind when first reading it far more than the fact
that my own unmethodical books were its subject-matter."
And soon after the appearance of the Hardy essay the editor
of the *Westminster Review*, Dr. Chapman, the one-time intimate of George Eliot, expressed the wish to meet him, accepted contributions, and put him in charge of the theological
and religious reviewing department of the paper, to which a
small salary was attached. Chapman died a few years later
and the Review dwindled, and H.E.'s chance of becoming
sub-editor came to nothing. He fell in with other editors of
the advanced type of paper such as *Mind* and *Today* which
were chiefly political, and H.E. found himself drawn into a
radical society called The Progressive Association for which
he became a self-effacing secretary and even compiled a little
book called *Hymns of Progress*, the only congregational
hymn-book in existence lacking any theological or theistic
tinge, and he wrote for it a hymn of his own, the first and last

stanza beginning with the words—"Onward, brothers, march
still onward."

It was inevitable that these activities should bring him in
touch with many of the interesting spirits of the day. One of
these was Thomas Davidson. Since he was neither a literary
artist nor a social reformer his name is known to few now.
He was a great talker, inspiring nearly all who listened to
him, easily gathering a band of young disciples. He was a
Scot with a deep knowledge and love for literature and
philosophy passionately fermenting within him, not in the
slightest degree diminished with advancing years. H.E. came
away from his first meeting with him feeling that he was the
most remarkable and intensely alive man he had ever met.
Davidson on his part was instantly attracted by H.E. and
was eager to gain his affection and allegiance. He was far
from being a holder-forth without listening to others, and was
most receptive to the ideas of his companions; but at times
when a group of them were together he would set forth his
own philosophic conceptions with memorable force and conviction and eloquence. H.E. was also a good listener. He
would sit in silence absorbing Davidson's view, and it would
appear that he was being carried along entirely with the
speaker. Yet this was by no means necessarily the case.
Davidson would find that while H.E. had sympathetically
absorbed the argument, he had completely failed to agree
with it. Thus, Davidson was very strong on Immortality—
which I think is a Scottish tendency among philosophers
shared even by the great modern Scot, W. Macneile Dixon,
author of *The Human Situation*. One evening he quoted Ten-
nyson's "In Memoriam" as a convincing argument in favour
of immortality. To H.E. who had studied the poem carefully
in his teens it was just a beautiful poem, the argument not
worth a moment's consideration: and he quoted Emerson
against Davidson. Davidson quoted Goethe against him, and
then fell back on the expression of his own fervent conviction
—but that was an argument which for H.E. *"carried not a
feather's weight."* This failure of his to be convinced by an-

other's conviction proved more than Davidson could bear. Later, in correspondence, he met with the same obstinate refusal of H.E. to take views second-hand. He was not firmly rooted enough himself to be able to stand this, and he ceased to write. He could receive nothing and stood in danger of losing what he possessed.

On the other hand he rendered H.E. a great service. Up till then he had thought that a given philosophical belief or system could be imparted from one person to another person; perhaps from a wise man to a seeker, or from a learned man to an ignorant one. Scraps of wisdom and chunks of information can be handed over thus, but not a philosophical system nor a way of life. Davidson somehow made this obvious to H.E. It was clear that Davidson's view of life, his pattern of beliefs, his convictions, were the outcome of the total person, his constitution, his nerves, his digestion, his manner of thought, his conscious and unconscious desires, his spiritual need, his upbringing, his environment, his own particular ecstasy on the mountain and agony in the garden. The outcome of all this, however well dressed up objectively and philosophically, cannot be shared by another, or if shared, is as unreal in the receiver as a literary style adopted from someone else. This was a valuable lesson to learn though it was the last thing Davidson desired to teach. And H.E. realized that the same could be said of any philosopher, and thus at this early age he was for ever freed, not from philosophy, but from philosophers. He saw that every man must create his own philosophy. This view does not make a well-presented philosophy any less splendid a thing than it was before, it places it in the category of art: a man who writes a great philosophy has written a great poem, as it were. Who could wish to do more than that? What better way do honour to the spirit of man, and inspire others in the art of life and thought? Years later when H.E. came to write *The Dance of Life*, this is his central point in his wonderful chapter on "The Art of Thinking," while in *Affirmations* in his essay on Nietzsche he had Davidson in mind when he wrote:

A noteworthy point in Nietzsche's conception of philosophy is his increasingly clear conception of its fundamentally psychological character. I mean to say that Nietzsche knows that a man's philosophy, to be real, must be the inevitable outcome of his own psychic constitution. It is a point that Philosophers have never seen. Perhaps Nietzsche was the first, however, hesitatingly, to realize it. It is only in the recognition of this fact that the eirenicon of philosophies—and one might add, of religions—can be found. The philosopher of old said: "This is *my* conception of the universe"; it was well. But he was apt to add: "It is *the* conception of the universe," and so put himself hopelessly in the wrong. It is as undignified to think another man's philosophy as to wear another man's cast-off clothes. Only the poor in spirit or in purse can find any satisfaction in doing either. A philosophy or religion can only fit the man for whom it was made. "There has only been one Christ," as Nietzsche put it, "and he died on the cross." But why waste energy in trying to manufacture a second Christian? We may be very sure that we can never find another Christian whom Christianity would fit so admirably as it once fitted Christ. Why not rest content with Christ? Let Brown be a Brownite and Robinson a Robinsonian. It is not good that they should exchange their philosophies, or that either should insist on thrusting his threadbare misfits on Jones, who prefers to be metaphysically naked. When men have generally begun to realize this the world will be a richer and honester world, and a pleasanter one as well. That Nietzsche had vaguely begun to realise it seems to me his chief claim to distinction in the purely philosophic field.

Does that last sentence seem hard to accept—that the distinction of a philosophy lies in the fact that it can only belong to its author. If that is so why bother to preach it? Yet why not? It is an inspiring thing. It can lift us upward as much as a great poem. By reading it and being stimulated as by the sunshine and the tempest and the waving corn, a man may find his own self and come into the way of salvation, he may catch sight of the Celestial City, nay, thus seize the sword with which to slay Apollyon.

8

THE spirit of Davidson had brought into existence another group called The Fellowship of the New Life. It
stood for a general urge towards socialism but more on the
ethical and humanitarian than the political side. Life must be
simplified, manual work combined with intellectual work, the
education of children put on a right basis, domestic life made
more co-operative, servants treated as friends, material things
subordinated to spiritual things, a personal effort must lead
to the higher life and the cultivation of a perfect character
in each and all, while everyone must remember Goethe's
motto and "be resolute to live in the Whole, the Good,
and the Beautiful." There is always some such Society in
ages of fermentation attracting many of the foremost spirits
of the day, and the only thing absent from this Pantisocratic
Scheme was a desire on the part of its members to leave the
imperfect environment and establish the perfect society on
the banks of the Susquehanna. It had also a political branch,
the members including Bernard Shaw and Sidney Webb who
soon broke away to form the historic Fabian Society, while
H.E., who had joined The New Fellowship at its conception,
though it is hard to associate him with perfectionist creeds
any more than with political aptitudes, remained with the
parent body until it peacefully expired in its sleep.

Davidson declared that he had never been attracted to anyone so much as to H.E. Later, when he gave up writing to him,

"I was content to make no attempt to continue the correspondence," says H.E., "much as Davidson had impressed me, I had never felt any response to his warm friendship." Cold words, and characteristic in a way, for one does not form the impression that he ever cared much for any man in a warm personal manner, though this may be due to his reserve in statement and the lack of high spirits in his personal sketches and in his letters to men—or to women, for that matter. He does show some warmth for Edward Carpenter to whom he was attached for forty years. The New Fellowship brought them together. At one of the meetings H.E. was sitting with his back to the door when turning round he saw "two brightly gleaming eyes out of the background of a quietly humourous face." It was Carpenter. It was sad to note how critics of the calibre of Desmond MacCarthy and E. M. Forster still belittled him at his centenary with the old gibe of "Whitman and lemonade" since *Towards Democracy* is nothing of the sort, while his *Art of Creation* and *Pagan and Christian Creeds* are still in front of the times. He had wide influence in his day and *Towards Democracy* will be read as long as true mystical works are treasured—that is, forever. It belongs to the department of literature which we call Scripture. Few have ever read Scripture on their own: I think fewer today than at any other time, now that we have entered the era when Bibles are discovered—*as literature*. There are not many English mystics, and Carpenter is one of the brightest and swiftest spirits whose light ever shone before men. It goes without saying that as soon as H.E. looked carefully into *Towards Democracy* he did not make the mistake of thinking it derivative of Whitman any more than in the sense that it was derivative of the earth and the sun. Edward Carpenter had another reason for being grateful to him. He was a sexual invert to some extent (though H.E. discerned no evidence of it) and was relieved to find a comprehender and a champion of the invert's right to existence.

H.E.'s connection with The New Fellowship led him forward to what was eventually to prove his main source of material support—work as editor of various series. Through his connections with the Fellowship he began to edit numerous volumes (including Landor's *Imaginary Conversations* for which he always had a high regard) for the "Camelot Series," while also beginning to write for *The Nineteenth Century* and *The Contemporary Review*, though he was determined to publish no book before the age of thirty. It was he who, after the "Camelot Series," was responsible for "The Mermaid Series" of the Elizabethan dramatists—volumes which I purchased in my twenties without much noting the Editor's Introductions. He was paid a salary, of course, though completely failing to get proper terms on account of his weak, almost irritating, lack of business ability. But when Fisher Unwin took over the Series from its original hands he suddenly dropped H.E. as editor, being shocked, it is supposed, by the manner in which he had failed to gloss over (thinking it unworthy to approach that great spirit with moral caveats) the charges of blasphemy and immorality brought against Marlowe. Thus the Series perished and was never superseded. H.E. went on to take a new Series which was at last to keep him going financially (not that I understand this) for the most critical twenty-five years of his life. This was "The Contemporary Science Series," though his taking it over was not till 1889. He proposed it himself and the financial backer instantly accepted the idea. He put the proposal forward just when approaching his final examinations in medicine and surgery. Imprudence, audacity, could scarcely go farther. Yet he knew, and never doubted, that he was taking absolutely the right step at the right moment—and in the event he did pass his medical examinations and became qualified. For all things work together for good for every man who trusts his star.

These projects, especially the editing of "The Mermaid Series," brought about a long-standing friendship with Arthur Symons. With this friend he often went abroad, his first journey being even at this time in 1881. He kept up his wanderings till 1925, visiting most of the continental countries, including Russia for which he formed a deep affection, though Spain was always to hold first place. These continental travels (how he found the time or the money remains a mystery) add richness to many of his books, especially *The Genius of Europe*. He did not make more than two journeys in his student days, one being in company with his schoolmaster friend, Mackay. This was to France, and on their way back they missed the evening boat-train at Rouen. Mackay was wildly exasperated and enraged. H.E. was unmoved, and gently guided Mackay to Dieppe where they spent a day which gave one of the most pleasant memories either of them was to hold. H.E. comments how on this occasion, as on others, it was his instinct to turn bad fortune into good fortune: "Again and again throughout life, in the largest matters as in small matters, I have built my success on a foundation of failure. I do not protest, I accept, but I create afresh." A great truth: and within the reach of every one of us.

It was in 1883 that in the course of his wide reading he came across a book called *The Story of an African Farm* by Olive Schreiner, and wrote a review of it in the *Indian Review* in a not uncritical spirit, being far from thinking too highly of it either in its art or its message. But he felt admiration for it and also thought that it had been neglected in the press. These feelings made him resolve to write to the author —unusual as such a proceeding was for him. It was an ordinary little act of sympathy, and it brought unlooked-for reward as such acts often do—since there is no friendmaker like the pen.

They arranged to meet at her Bayswater lodging house. Always rather childlike, she expected to meet a man who would look her straight in the eye and talk brilliantly, and on finding the reality different she retired into another room to cry, while he felt neither depression nor exaltation, though noting her shapeless clothes, her sturdy frame, and her large watchful eyes. But they soon grew on one another and it was not long before she was calling him her "other self." For his part he regarded her as one of the most wonderful women of her time, and it gave him immense satisfaction to think that she should be the first woman he was to know intimately. Even so, he withheld himself. He made no advances. He scarcely ever did. Thus he met with no repulses. When Miss Schreiner first wanted to kiss him he was unaware of it, and next time she was obliged to make it more obvious.

This was the period of the New Woman. It is not a misnomer. The superficies really was new, however old as the hills the things underneath. She was newer than the women of today, and she felt new, rebelling as she was and beating up against the ghastly Victorian age—(always symbolised for me by the picture of a normal Victorian bathing party when rather more clothes were put on to go into the water than for remaining on land). The spirit of the new age encouraged such a person as Olive Schreiner to fulfil herself to the utmost, and while being a woman of great intelligence and high ideals was also a child and a savage in the best sense, ready to receive and indeed seeking the man who would tempestuously sweep her off her feet and pass perhaps beyond any conventional code of morality. For a brief period it seemed to her possible that H.E. was the man she was looking for. And he in his turn allowed the idea of marriage to cross his mind. It is easy to see how he could have deceived himself and her at this stage, and have had an exciting time, however temporary it might prove. But he never did anything in a hurry, and it was not in his nature to allow self-gratification or the gratification of others to interfere with ultimate aims. He did not disguise from her the fact that he had not it in him to satisfy her elemental primitive nature, and she speedily recognized this—possibly aided thereto by the fact that when once she came from the bathroom completely naked into the sitting-room where he was waiting, to expound an idea which had just occurred to her, he concentrated on the idea.

In the end they understood each other very well. She may

have got him wrong in some respects, imagining him to be "a man of the study" which was so far from the truth, but she told him that his call was to literature and not to medicine, while also she told him that his scientific side would save him. She was a great stimulus to him in finding himself, and so was he to her. They loved each other deeply, and remained lovers, though not technically so—which I emphasize however much that statement may annoy readers who bank everything upon the sexual act. When they were apart they wrote to each other daily, sometimes twice daily (as did Shaw and Ellen Terry at nearly the same time), so intimate were they in the non-police-court sense. When back in Africa, she wrote—"I wish I could see you, my brother, my dear one, who has loved me more truly and faithfully than anyone." And fifteen years after both of them were married she wrote—"I believe if I heard you were dangerously ill I should start off to England at once, if I had to borrow the money and knew I was likely to die on the way." I think we may call this love.

These varied interests and activities were subordinate to his main task of pursuing his medical studies and becoming qualified. He did too many other things to allow a brilliant student career, not his line in any case, but he was an orderly, punctual student in his attendances and was conscientious when "clerk" or "dresser," while in one department he actually secured a Certificate of Honour, for Midwifery, "having satisfactorily carried out the duties of visiting accoucheur during three separate fortnights in three successive years, although only one fortnight was demanded for the whole course." Most students were satisfied with the arduousness and discomforts of the regulation fortnight, but H.E. welcomed more on account of the work coming within the sphere of sex and because it gratified that interest in women, scientific and emotional, which was part of his nature. Nor was he easily overcome with squeamishness at the trying experience, though some of his colleagues when on their first case were known to faint.

St. Thomas's Hospital stood near an area which in those days was largely of slum character. The midwifery clerk would hold himself in readiness, and there would be about two calls during the twenty-four hours, when he would have to go, generally in the night, through dark and narrow streets to some humble dwelling into a sordid room full of bugs and fleas. H.E.'s first call was to a woman who lay in a drunken stupor on a filthy bed; and he was able to recall only one childbirth—out of the hundred in his experience—which was easy.

He had not yet obtained his full qualification by 1886, but it was in order for students in those days to act sometimes as unqualified assistant to a doctor. Before he passed his finals he went in this way first to a doctor in the north of Lancashire, and then in the follow-year to Blackburn, thus getting to know and to like the Lancashire people whom he met in their homes. When his time came for him to leave he found that he had caught a fever, and the family he was with pressed him to delay his departure, but this he declined, not wishing to miss an exhibition of Old Masters at Burlington House. On reaching home it was clear that he had a fairly severe attack of scarlet fever. His mother looked after him, but by the time he was getting better she had caught it. He was well enough to attend to her when the nurse was out. One morning he came and sat in her room by the fireside and began to read in a German version Ibsen's *Peer Gynt* for the first time. He came to that remarkable scene when Peer enters the hut in which his mother lies dying with the fire on the hearth and the old tom-cat on the stool, and Peer talks to her in the tone of the days of his childhood, lulling her to death with the same stories that she had once lulled him to sleep. As H.E. sat there lost in this scene, he heard the sound of difficult breathing coming from his own mother, and saw a slight convulsion pass over her features. Then there was nothing and he saw that she was dead, and he knew that his early return had meant her sentence of death. "I stood beside her for a little while. I had had many experiences of the diseases and sufferings of strangers in the hospital and elsewhere, but the first person whose death I had ever witnessed was the nearest person to me in all the world. Then I quickly went from the room and lay on my bed, ready to tell the nurse, so soon as she returned, what had happened."

9

IN 1889 he obtained his M.D.—the Licentiate in Medicine, Surgery, and Midwifery of the Society of Apothecaries. This had meant some slight slowing down of his literary activities. Even so he was editing the "Contemporary Science Series," and in 1888 suddenly conceived and carried out what he rightly calls a *tour de force*. He prepared to write a book on criminal anthropology. As I have already said, when I came to him first I was unable to understand how this could have been his first book, and I had no inclination to open it till now. The fact is he was walking along the Strand one day and came to a favourite bookstall where he saw Tarde's *La Criminalité Comparée*. He had never dreamt of writing a book on criminals nor did he know there was such a subject as criminal anthropology. He read the book eagerly, came upon the great Italian, Lombroso, and instantly resolved to write upon the subject himself. I do not give that as the explanation, only as the occasion that fired him; all we can say is that his investigation-genius was waiting for an opportunity —and here was one. He set to work in a thoroughly professional manner, obtaining the required books and periodicals (mostly in Italian and inaccessible in England), started lines of investigation and enquiry in various directions, circulating printed questions to medical officers of prisons, and so on. In a year he had mastered the material and in 1890 published *The Criminal*—though it was in 1889 that he took his final medical examinations! The book attracted wide attention not only on account of its comprehensive survey but because of the advocated reforms, some of which have now been realized, though others, such as the idea that a man going to prison for theft, say, should no more be given a definite sentence than a man sent to a mental hospital, have not caught on.

The book is largely out of date now, I understand, though I have not the smallest qualification to pass an opinion on this aspect. I would have been glad to have found it dull and unnecessary to read, but it held me throughout by its interest and gruesome detail. I was also fascinated by the scientific manner of going at the subject, the grouping, the statistics, the references, the felicity with which he examined the dicta such as "every society has the criminals it deserves" since much crime like infanticide, is related to the social factor, while the relation of crimes against the person and the price of alcohol, and between crimes against property and the price of wheat, can be subject to statement. And since the book was written by H.E. I should have expected things unlikely to appear elsewhere in this kind of book, such as a quotation from Homer and a reference to the face of Socrates which a Greek physiognomist judged to be brutal, sensuous, and inclined to drunkenness—a disposition which Socrates admitted was natural to him, although he had overcome it. Perhaps I should also have expected some amusement when he deals with the biological beginnings of crime. Thus Lombroso claimed that certain insectivorous plants belonged to the category of criminals. H.E. doubted this classification as tenable since an act common to a whole species could not reasonably be termed criminal. To be criminal the deed must be exceptional in the species, provoking social reaction among other members of that species. Thus we "could scarcely hope to find genuine vegetable criminals, even among the parasites." Among animals he thought it possible to find criminals in the technical sense—for example rogue elephants outlawed by their own kind. Turning to the lower races of man, we have to tread carefully, he suggests, on ruling criminality, even when an act such as parricide is involved, and keep our indignation in check, since the distance between ourselves and even the lowest races is quite measurable. "Our social code is not far removed from that of the Maori who considered that it was murder to kill the man to whom he had given hospitality, but not murder to run his spear through the stranger whom he met on his morning walk. We today regard it as a great crime to kill our own fathers and children; but even the most civilized European nation—whichever that may be—regards it as rather glorious to kill the fathers and children of others in war. We are not yet able to grasp the relationship between men." Finally, I think it should be added that, however out of date this book may be in some respects, it is far from out of date in its comprehension, and therefore, compassion—which most of us need to exercise on this subject.

In the same year he produced *The New Spirit*. He had long previously fixed on thirty as the proper age to publish his first book. Few writers can plan their lives, but H.E. did on a generous scale, and stuck to his plan, and this may be one of the reasons why his life itself seems such a work of art. Thus on his thirtieth year he brought out two books of such an entirely different kind that anyone ignorant of their authorship would scarcely concede the possibility that they could both be written by the same man.

When I first picked up *The New Spirit* in my twenties it made no impression on me. I was much too immature. It contains essays on Diderot, Heine, Ibsen, Whitman, and Tolstoy, and I could not then see that he was both a Diderot, the Encyclopaedist, and a Whitman, the Answerer. Moreover, at that time I was under the influence of Bernard Shaw. I hasten to add that I shall always be grateful for that influence, and while I no longer look to him for profundity as a sage, I shall ever revere him for his understanding of human beings, and the lack of falsity in his plays either in terms of character or action or speech—and I believe that this is what will be fully recognized when his death-centenary comes round. Being under the spell of his rhythm I could not at that time adapt myself to the different rhythm of H.E. whose approach, in any case, nowhere comes within the focus of the Shavian mind. Also I could never have grasped his thought at that age. It always takes me a long time to make a new angle (it took me years to grasp what Whitman was saying). H.E. seldom uses long words, jargon never, nor is there anything involved in his expression; but sometimes the subtlety of his thought is so great that it makes demands upon the reader not easily obeyed. You have to realize where he is standing. His last chapter, "Conclusion," in *The New Spirit* is as packed a piece as anything he ever wrote. Every year it gets slightly more up to date. We are catching up on him. It is not easy. I have just re-read it four times. After trying to see if it were subject to a brief statement I gave up the attempt: it is too pregnant— and his *slant* should not be spoilt by me. This much may be said: supposing the reader is a person who no longer responds to creeds but does not care for the negativity of agnosticism; here is help. I will suppose that the reader is familiar with the present conception of matter and mind, and perhaps has studied Bertrand Russell's wonderful essay in his latest book, *Portraits from Memory*, called "Mind and Matter." Having formed the impression that there is very little difference between mind and matter in the modern view, the reader may become uncertain as to where he stands in relation to religion. Russell does not answer this question, for his mind does not move beyond his chosen field, and indeed could only do so if it had experience of any further field—and he seldom deceives himself or his readers. He has given us the scientific attitude towards reality, and professes to do no more (though he does not, I think, allow that more could be done).

Here is H.E.

The scientific attitude has a series of implications of its own. In its solvents all things are analysed and anatomized; the 'soul' of our religious world—the vast pulsating centre, at the bottom of which, according to the profound saying of the old mystic, lies the unutterable sigh which we call God—is resolved into a momentary focus of ever-shifting rays of force; it is but an incident in a huge evolution of shifting forces which we may, if we like, personify as Nature, but which, none the less, we cannot conceive as a whole. The scientific attitude has its own implications, and their far-reaching significance, their immense value for the individual and for the race, can scarcely be overrated.

That was written in 1890, some fifty years before it was generally understood by the learned that a chair is not an object, not even a changing object, but an event. Now, it is possible that some readers may be far from pleased with that quotation. Here is H.E. calmly accepting the view that science resolves the soul into shifting rays of force, and he seems quite happy about it. Where does religion come in? If that is all we have there is no place for religion, he may think. But it is *not* all we have. *It is just one of the responses which man makes to the universe:* it is the intellectual response, the motion to find out and reason out how things work; it is the scientific response. But that is not the only motion which man makes as he stands confronted by the universe. Emotion is called forth also. This is quite a different response. It takes in the Whole thing and values it instead of examining the machinery. This response discovers different terms, such as Beauty and Love. This is religion. Is it not clear that neither of these motions which have been called forth by the play of the universe upon its creature Man, can be put out of countenance by the other? Is not this obvious? He stands there responding in many different ways—in thought, or in grief, or in ecstasy, or in fear. None of these findings can claim exclusive Truth. It is only the fanaticism of narrowness and ignorance of the *total human situation* that can suggest conflicts between these responses. Some men *are* wholly scientific in their motion; they have no need for the religious motion or no call for it, and should be perfectly content, and often are. Some men *are* wholly emotional in their response, all scientific motion is absent, and they too should be perfectly content, and often are. But what sense is there in quarrelling and taking sides since both parties possess legitimate data which

nothing can discountenance? "But for a little while we are allowed to enter the house of life," says H.E. in "The Conclusion," "and gather around its fire. Why pull each other's hair
and pinch each other's arms like naughty children? Well
would it be to warm ourselves at the fire together, to clasp
hands, to gain all the joy that comes of comradeship, before
we are called out, each of us, into the dark, alone."

As soon as he had completed these tasks, the publishing of
the books and the passing of his medical examinations, he
went with Arthur Symons for three months to Paris where he
appears to have met many of the chief artists of the day, including Verlaine, Rodin, Huysmans, Élie Reclus, and Remy
de Gourmont. When in England he never cared to meet people, but he loved France and Paris, and had soaked himself in
French literature, and he seems to have been willing to enter a
Parisian *salon*. Even so there is no suggestion that when in
Paris he shone in company any more than he did in England.
But he appears to have felt an attachment to Verlaine, a deep
respect for him as a man, and as a gentleman, also regarding
him as one of the few essential poets France has produced,
while the one writer with whom he says he formed a permanent tie was the great critic Remy de Gourmont—though the
Frenchman who has written about him best is Élie Reclus.
He regarded this sojourn in Paris as the climax of this early
period of his life, the fitting climax of his thirtieth year in
which he had completed the long medical training so necessary for his own mission as he saw it; in which he had published his first two books in totally different spheres, each giving him a reputation (very rare for the first books of any
considerable writer); in which he had initiated the "Contemporary Science Series" that was to support him (for he
never practised as a doctor to any extent); in which his
mother had died and he had now rooms of his own; in which
Olive Schreiner, having done much for him, had gone off-
stage, back to Africa. "My apprenticeship to life was over.
I was master of myself and my life." The clock had been

wound up. The machine had been created to perform its work in the world. I hope I have at least suggested how it was wound up. Now the mighty spring could be liberated. That is an image he uses himself in his memorable "Open Letter to Biographers" for whom he felt no undue regard, considering that they did not always know what their chief business was. After this winding-up process we can expect the deeds to follow, whether they be "the assault of great fortresses or the escalade of mighty sentences. There is the same heroic effort and achievement whether on the walls of Jerusalem when Godfrey scaled them or on Flaubert's sofa at Rouen."

I would add, however, living in modern times, this winding-up takes place between nineteen and thirty. How lucky are they who do not inherit just at that time some war which will take four to six years of their life away, and perhaps make it impossible for them ever to get going. Like Bernard Shaw and other "last of the great Victorians" Havelock Ellis was not imprisoned at killable age to make a sergeant-major's holiday and to qualify for the kind of hero so vastly different from him who will undertake the escalade of mighty sentences.

10

THUS he was in high spirits at the age of thirty, "master of himself and of his life." Would he remain master? Or would he yield to a woman and lose his freedom? He did yield to a woman. But he did not lose his freedom nor swerve from his path.

Edith Lees, whom he married, has not worn well. She was one of those people who on paper become smaller than they were in life. H.E. has given such an all-round account of her in his Autobiography that we see her with extraordinary clarity. Yet since we cannot see her in the flesh, it is hard to feel her as the wonderful woman which she clearly was. Her exasperating qualities come between us and her, and we do not hear her ringing laugh and voice. On paper, whether revealed by H.E. or by herself in her books, essays, and lectures,[1] she is hardly sympathetic; the living woman is not there. Some people have spoken of the martyrdom of H.E. to his wife. I think they are mistaken. It is true that to a certain extent he had to play the martyr and the saint, but what harm is there in that if the hero can do it? If he can it will be a pity if he marries a cushion. H.E. had much to be thankful for. Though a born bachelor in many ways, he had a great capacity for love, and could not have satisfied himself with promiscuity. Edith did not sit on top of him. She did not insist that he be with her al-

[1] These consist of: *Kit's Woman; Attainment; My Cornish Neighbours; James Hinton: Essays & Lectures.*

ways. She left him alone when he needed solitude—she found solitary places for him. She did not make finance a nightmare —not often. She did not burden him with a household of children. She allowed him, even encouraged him, *to do his work.* These are great virtues. He had to pay, of course; for love, on whatever scale, in whatever mode, always commands the just price.

The Fellowship of the New Life brought them together. It was in 1887 that they were introduced on a country excursion. Neither of them was much impressed with the other. She was put off by his ill-fitting clothes. He disliked her pale blue eyes. He made a joke which didn't come off, for she was over-serious then. It was two or three years before they met again. In 1890 someone gave her a copy of *The New Spirit.* (Nearly thirty years later, just before her death she declared that when "I first read *The New Spirit* I knew I loved the man who wrote it." But I do not think she did know this at the time.) In the same year she went to stay the night at Lamorna in Cornwall at the house of Miss Agnes Jones. It so happened that this lady was a friend of H.E., for she was a disciple of James Hinton (once more he comes in decisively), and she told Edith Lees that she was expecting Havelock Ellis that afternoon. Miss Lees was annoyed. In spite of *The New Spirit* she professed to feel that she would rather not meet the author again. She went upstairs and explained this to a faithful servant, Ellen Taylor, who (strange as it must seem to our period) accompanied her on her walking tours. But Ellen's feet were sore and she pleaded for a quiet rest.

So they met again. This time they established some sincerity and intimacy. Later in the week when he had gone to St. Ives, it happened that she was in a cobbler's shop having her shoes done, and caught sight of him in the street. She instantly ran out in her stockinged feet, calling out to him in a clear ringing voice. They returned to the shop, waited for the shoes, and then went on together. They became closer friends. She was ready now to discover the person beneath the exterior which at first had failed to attract her since her ideal man was a

lady's man, a well-tailored, correct, compliment-paying, gal-
lant man of the world—not a type found in excess among the
Fellowship of the New Life. His ideal woman, as a literary
man's wife, contained some of the properties of a feather-bed.
She was nervous, restless, irritable, impulsive, irresponsible.
Men and women do not often marry their opposites, but still
less often their ideal.

A few days later, after leaving St. Ives, she wrote a hasty
note telling him where she was and hinting that he might look
her up. True to form, and to the technique (entirely unconscious) of walking smartly in the opposite direction when
Love calls so that Love may pursue, he did not look her up.
Nevertheless he got in touch with her when back in London,
and she would frequently run in to see him in his rooms in
Paddington, generally "in a hurry," and thus stay long. He
never went to her rooms in Wigmore Street. No thought of
love arose between them—or so he says. Then one day she
confided that she had been in love with a certain member of
the Fellowship, who did not return it and now he had left
England. This was rare with her, since her passionate attractions were for women. But it often happens that women who
fall in love with women, and men who fall in love with men
are also anxious to have a normal relationship with a member
of the opposite sex. It was certainly so in the case of Edith
Lees. But at this time he was naturally unaware of this aspect
of her constitution.

Her father was a Lancashire man, her mother from Cheshire. Many people regarded her as Celtic, and thought that
she was Irish, on account of her vivacious qualities (and according to H.E. there is supposed to be much ancient Celtic
blood in Cheshire). Perhaps I may say in passing, as an Irishman on both sides, that I do not recognize vivacity as a
particularly Celtic trait: the Irish are a melancholy people,
though they seek to disguise their sadness—hence your "funny
Irishman," and the Irish drama of comi-tragedy. Any Irish
traits which Edith Lees possessed came from her mother, a
woman, it is recorded, of singular charm. She died shortly

after the birth of her only child, and was worshipped by that child thereafter. She hated her father. He had inherited from his miserly and tyrannical grandfather a good deal of money, but could only lose money himself. He was a morbid, eccentric, angular, irritable, unhealthy, and cruel man, equally adept at hurting others or himself. He attempted to break-in his daughter much as if she had been an excitable mare. It had the opposite effect and made her break out, and form a deep resentment against men and a life-long determination never to be dominated or ordered about by them. Her father married again and her step-mother treated her to cutting sneers which were returned with interest—a competition which served to sharpen early in life a tongue naturally given to sarcasm and exaggeration. This was an imperfect home-life for a girl who was wayward, egotistic, melodramatic, eager for the lime-light, and as easily hurt as she was ready to love. Her father sent her to a convent and soon she wanted to become a Catholic and to be a nun. He snatched her from there as a brand from the burning and sent her to a school with a headmistress of free-thinking opinions. She was twenty-one when her father died, and quickly spent the little money he left, after which she tried to run a school, anticipating, as throughout life in other instances, speedy and complete success. It failed, and she found herself in debt, and had a nervous breakdown. She was rescued by friends. It is not surprising, for she had a genius for friendship: H.E. says that he never knew anyone who had so many friends. Two came forward now, one to nurse her back to health (she was a person who often got ill and swiftly recuperated from illness), the other to tide her over the financial disaster. She belonged to the company of those who gratefully remember kindness and help; and all her life she never ceased to revere these friends.

It will be seen that if like ever does "call to like" it was not so in this case. H.E. was an exceedingly quiet man, a dreamer, slow, reserved, a lover of solitude and a man of few friends, incapable of even the smallest amount of small talk at a social gathering, while the nearest he got to giving a public performance was reading the minutes of the last meeting as secretary of The Progressive Society. He had such an immense range of intellectual and artistic interests and works that it might have been, that like some other warriors, he would find no time for woman save as relaxation. Yet this was not so. For him the art of living seemed the greatest of the arts, and with it the art of loving. It is not strange that he felt drawn towards this woman who so vibrated with life. And it is not strange that she should have felt drawn towards a man who could give her peace, and who, perhaps of all men in all the world, would try to understand her.

Moreover they shared views on marriage. He felt that he would never be able to support her financially. She was sincerely determined on independence. (They both had about the same income.) They agreed that finances should be shared equally—though in the event (need it be said) she "borrowed" on a considerable scale with the sincere intention of repaying it in due course—without doing so. Surprisingly this seems to have surprised H.E. In the end he found that it came rather more expensive this way than if he had always taken care of all the finances. Again, so far from either of them being determined on the double-bed they preferred double houses—though they were often together. They were also agreed that it would be unwise to have children. He felt that on his side it might never be economically possible. On her side her doctor held the view that, on account of hereditary tendencies, if she should marry she certainly ought not to have children. He was kind enough to tell her that he believed that she would never find her way into a lunatic asylum, but that if she were to enter one she would never come out again—and in the end this was a close thing. They both regarded marriage as "sacred and inviolable"—high words for life sentence. The question was therefore, could they risk it? A free union did not appeal to them: and in this I think they were influenced by their friend Eleanor Marx (daughter of Karl Marx) who had formed a free union which ended in mutual suicide.

It was a courtship conducted under no romantic illusions, in some sense rather reminiscent of the Carlyles. It was largely carried out by letter, a correspondence course in courtship which might commend itself to a woman's journal since there was so much striving on both sides to get to know each other before taking the step. "It's very pathetic when one thinks of it," he writes, "that people think it wrong and unnatural for two persons to learn to know each other before they think of binding themselves together for ever. Marry *first*, and then you may be free to find out that you've chosen the wrong person! One realizes how that sort of pressure works on weak young creatures and leads to so much misery."

At length on December 19th, 1891 they were married in a Registry Office at Paddington, after which they returned to their respective bachelor homes. There was no wedding breakfast, though they both had some porridge. She invited her host of friends to an At Home in the afternoon at the Fellowship House. He was obliged to put in an appearance but was allowed to arrive late. Next morning they went to Paris. Knowing and loving the city so well he saw to it that she had a time worth remembering. One hour remained in his memory above others. They went to a concert to hear Beethoven's Ninth Symphony. He recalls—"I shall never forget, and never know again the rapture which I experienced. In the exaltation of that solemn hymn to Joy my own new personal life seemed to blend harmoniously with the vision of my mission of work in the world. This realization shone radiantly out of my eyes, and in much later years Edith would still sometimes describe my face as she saw it then. I have heard the Ninth Symphony since, but I never again recaptured the rapture of that moment."

When they returned to London he went back to his rooms in Paddington, she to the Fellowship House. Soon they worked out a plan of existence. They spent the winters together in Cornwall and the summers largely apart. Here we see the son following in the steps of his father who had always maintained two establishments, one for himself, the ship, and one for his wife on land. The wives of sailors are generally content with this arrangement: there is no cause for gossip among neighbours, while the husband is kept out of mischief. It was less easy for Edith Ellis whose husband was not a sailor of ordinary seas. True, she had declared before marriage that she wouldn't mind a bit this *modus vivendi*, that it was just what she wanted, and so on. It turned out that she really wanted two things: to have him with her and at the same time to satisfy her expansive sociability by inviting to the house a succession of visitors. He found this impossible. He was obliged to seek rest and peace not only from her exhausting restlessness but from her host of friends. There was no other way out. She came to realize this, and accepted it.

While this plan solved one problem it brought another. I do not think that the one which it brought can be compared with the importance of solving his working-conditions problem. Indeed it was another factor which helped to promote the carrying out of his work—and perhaps a biographer of Havelock Ellis may be pardoned for looking at things from his point of view in this connection. She often had a stream of friends coming to see her. Yet not always, of course. There were occasions when she was left alone after he had gone. On one of these occasions, quite soon after their marriage, she was joined by an old friend named Claire with whom she now suddenly formed a passionate attachment. H.E. was aware that as a schoolgirl she had formed love attachments to other girls just as most boys do for boys. He had no real practical knowledge of inborn sexual inversion of character such as he now discovered in his wife. He had perceived nothing of the masculine traits in her, and, for that matter, to the end never regarded her as really man in any degree but always as "woman, boy, and child," in almost equal measure.

As soon as she began to experience this new emotional outflow she wrote to tell him of it with trustful confidence. It came as a surprise to him. At first he did not receive it with equanimity. The actual fact of the homosexual trait did not upset him, for in her case he knew that there would be nothing ugly or ignoble about it. But he could scarcely help feeling that this absorption in another person would mean a diminution of her feelings for him. Yet as she had written to him in the absolute belief that she could rely upon his comprehension and love, "as if to a divine being superior to the weaknesses of a human husband," he overcame his feelings and gave her the response she desired. This was not good policy. A little later she wrote him a letter so foolish and so complacent that it did draw from him a strong protest. When she realized that she had gone too far she was horrified. She thought she had lost his love and revealed how much she loved him. Instantly his mind was set at peace. He was never again jealous on this score. He no longer minded her frequent passions for women friends, while nothing could exceed her gratitude to him for his understanding, and she felt, as she was frequently to feel throughout her life at lucid moments, that it was a miracle that she had found *him*, the only man in the world likely to understand her or even stand her—a fact which he himself regarded as no less than the truth.

Soon he had further cause not to be troubled about this. In this same year of 1893 his wife, having no servant sleeping in a bungalow they had rented at Haslemere, wanted a companion when he was away. He suggested a young woman he had known since childhood, called Amy. She agreed to come. She had always cherished a secret love for H.E. from a distance, for she was not a person of any pretensions. He had overlooked this gentle, quiet girl in the well known manner of the young intellectual and idealist. He now became aware of her qualities. He perceived value in the sweet, soothing, and unselfish traits which she possessed. One day when he had gone for a walk with her and they had sat on a fallen tree-trunk together, he gave her a kiss—exactly one, of the simplest kind. She was a little slow: he was slower—and some years passed before he gave her a second kiss. But he kept back nothing from his wife, not even this first kiss. She took it badly. It did not occur to her that while it was his job to understand her irregularities it might be hers to understand his. She stormed. She raved. She created painful scenes. She sneered at Amy's "femininity." This was unwise. Amy re-

mained self-effacingly silent, while he eloquently refrained
from saying what might have been said. In the absence of
such scenes the situation might have melted into nothingness.
As it was his feelings for Amy were stimulated. The kiss became a germ. When he was in London his relations with her
grew closer, for she lived in the suburbs. He still concealed
nothing from Edith, and there was more resentment and
more scenes. He felt that the situation had become intolerable
and he resolved to terminate his relations with Amy. She retired to the continent. But this resolution was not a solution.
Nothing was solved: no sooner was he completely cut off
from Amy than his dejection alarmed his wife. She saw it was
useless to expect him to persist in the effort. He had made the
effort, and that was something; she decided to accept the situation, and did so, though not without occasional revulsions
and outbursts of bitterness during many years. She would declare that Amy lacked either the strength of character or
mental ability to enter their lives. But he got all that he
needed in this line from Edith. He also wanted quietness, and
this he received from Amy. Edith herself needed peace, and
she got it from her husband, while she could expend her in-
tenseness upon Claire and others who were to follow. I have
heard it said that if only H.E. had not left her alone at the
beginning she might never have taken up with Claire or anyone else. I think this view is mistaken. If a person is a genuine
invert and really does fall in love with the same sex, this is not
something that can be altered though it might be suppressed.
If she had suppressed it he would never have been able to cope
with so intense and restless a person all the time. As it was
these women friends took her off his hands and he could do
his work. In this way the difficulties on both sides were faced
and overcome. In the process their marital relationship in the
narrow sense was brought to an end. They came to feel that
they were unsuited in this, and that they could develop better without it. Once, later, she suddenly suggested that they
go back to their early relations. He allowed the proposal to
drop without discussion. It was never brought up again.

It might seem from this brief account that their marriage was a failure, and that I am attempting to conceal the fact. Yet it is quite plain from his account and from her letters that it was very far from being a failure—if passionate devotion between two people for over thirty years is the criterion. We will have more to notice about this as we go along. After mentioning the dropping of the strictly marital relationship, this is what H.E. has to say early in his story:

It is, I know, not uncommon, almost indeed the rule, after some years of married life, for the passion with which it may have begun to die down into calm friendship or cool indifference, or worse. With us the real love—it was scarcely passion—gave place to none of these things. On the contrary it grew; it grew into passion, and this more than a spiritual passion since the yearning tenderness of the body was not excluded. Only one thing was left out, a real and definite thing, yet so small in comparison to all that was left that we scarcely missed it. Even years after her death and all was in seeming over, I would find myself exclaiming inwardly: My sweetheart!

The greatest of all my revelations which my life with Edith brought me was this discovery that not only affection but the deepest passion of love can exist and develop continuously even when the relationship of sex in the narrow sense has ceased to exist. That it may require some such relation for its foundation I believe. But what I have learnt is that passionate love—that is to say a love deeper and more intimately moving than simple affection—may continue for ever in its absence and stir the heart long years after the woman who inspired it is dead. I know by experience that love can last as long as we last. I know how it is that in old days when they expected to live again they said that love is eternal, I can understand that threefold sigh of joy over a dead lover: *Amavimus Amamus Amabimus.*

11

AT FIRST they took a little place called the Cot at Carbis Bay in Cornwall, and they were to live in this district for many years—though H.E. did not spend much of the summers there, and seems, strangely, to have favoured London at this time of year. One day Edith suddenly announced that she had taken over the Count House. It was a gloomy building, once the official headquarters of a mine, and it would never have occurred to him to live in such a place—but he was not consulted, and never was on such occasions. However, it had a beautiful outlook over sea and moor, and in her hands became a fairly comfortable home. The chief reason for her wish to take it was that she had a strong desire to farm. To a reader of today this may seem a not unusual impulse for a woman. It was unusual for a young lady of the 'nineties. In any case it generally remains an impulse. At all times it is a desperate venture if the onus of responsibility is assumed. As one who knows a little of what is involved in agriculture—though my experience was only for six years, and without responsibility—I must venture to say that her activities at this time were remarkable, and lend support to H.E.'s assertion that while she was prone to catch diseases (from which she made swift recoveries) she was also robust and physically strong. For many years she got right down to earth, and I think that this should be clearly remembered by anyone who may feel equal—as I do not—to make an assessment of her character and gifts.

She succeeded in creating quite a reasonable little farm out of the place. She began with a few small fields and later added more. She began with one cow, Miranda, procured from a neighbouring farmer who named all his cows after Shakespearian heroines, and added more later. There were two donkeys and a horse, together with pigs, fowls, and ducks, and an enormous assortment of dogs and cats. Soon she needed staff in order to cope, and engaged a man, a dairy-woman, and two servants in the house, cook and housemaid —for these were the days when you hardly paid anyone anything for this kind of work, and when you could buy a solid meal for one and sixpence. In any case Edith was one of those persons who easily got people to work for them, being interested in everyone and free and easy with everyone in contrast to the stiff, prim, undemocratic Englishwoman of her day. She knew nothing of agriculture before this; and yet, such was the rapidity of her intelligence, that she did not make serious mistakes in this trickiest of all crafts! She liked to be able to do anything, including ploughing; she took over the poultry entirely; she bred pigs, and was sometimes discovered by startled visitors from Kensington cutting up carcasses into the required joints for customers. She made hay for the stock, and cultivated flowers and vegetables. H.E. was a spectator of all this. At ease with Nature, he was yet no agriculturalist. He did not love the spade. She did—for a time. "I shall never forget," he says, "how one morning after dressing, I wandered to the window of her study and came suddenly upon the vision of her below, spade in hand, vigorously digging up potatoes, with almost a fever of exhilaration, her face radiantly beautiful in its animated joy."

After they had moved into the Count House she proceeded to let furnished the Cot and three other cottages taken over for the purpose—and again he knew little of the matter till it was virtually settled. An extraordinary assortment of ten-ants seem to have rented these premises from time to time, suburbanites and subtopians, artists, men of letters, victims of alcohol and drugs, soldiers, diplomats, foreign professors, runaway couples, Russian Counts, and clever adventurers, all of whom proved remunerative consumers of agricultural products. The farm worked for at least ten years—which, in my opinion, is a creditable performance. Then she began to flag. The kind of person who is radiant about lifting potatoes is never *very* long on the land, and she began to want to write books and give lectures—and you cannot do literary work if you are in a responsible position in farming, however small the scale. When this time came—to make a chronological anticipation—a speculator decided to re-open the mine (tin, I suppose, being in Cornwall), and required the Counting House for its original purpose. But Edith held the lease. The Company offered her ten pounds to clear out. She demanded two hundred. The Company paid—and then failed in its mining scheme. However, this brought the farming to an end. They disposed of the greater part of the impedimenta; but the question remained as to what was to be done with an old horse and its inseparable companion, a donkey, born on the farm and with an exceedingly amiable disposition though with an insatiable weakness for cigarettes. Nothing would induce Edith to part with them. Wherever she went they had to follow. She even brought them to London, and it was a great nuisance supplying oats for the horse and cigarettes for the donkey.

Before she went in for the farming activities she set herself to find H.E. a suitable place to work. And she did discover an ideal spot in the immediate neighbourhood. It was a rough little building which had once been a mining shed at a place called Hawkes Point in the middle of the bay. It was an isolated retreat overlooking the sea, which commanded, according to Edward Carpenter who came to see it, the finest view on the whole English coast. Apart from the hut, made into quite a comfortable studio for him by Edith, a boat had been set on end against the hillside, which made an ivy-covered shelter facing the sea, in which he could write or read whenever the weather allowed—which in Cornwall was sometimes during the whole of the winter. In this shelter, or in the studio, he worked in complete freedom from distraction for ten or twelve years. "If I owed nothing more to Edith," he rightly and justly says, "than the opportunity to obtain and to preserve these conditions in the happiest manner possible my debt to her would still be immense." He can never have written truer or more heart-felt words.

He had always preferred to write and read in the open air if possible, and here he was able to achieve this for years in perfect conditions. This is an important aspect of the man. His work does not smell of the lamp, it smells of the earth, it smells of the sea, and partakes of the salt of the sea. And how, one may ask in passing, can any man *really* write sanely about Nature, and Nature's specialty, Man, unless he is set in the midst of Nature straightly confronted by the scheme? In the middle of the study we may not, for instance, be able to accept the "problem of evil" or that red tooth and that red claw; but in the middle of the sea, or under the sea peering through Beebe's window, or on the plain, or in the wood, or from the mountain-top, we see that there is no problem and that all things are all things, members one of another, so that when one becomes another by being eaten, and that when the fly catches the gnat, and the gnat the microbe, and this fish that fish, all is well, and that when the "Red slayer thinks he slays, And the slain thinks he is slain" [1] both are making a gross error. Very few British writers can work continuously out of doors, the temperature and the wind making it far from easy. Yet this was certainly the practice of H.E. and also of Edward Carpenter. H.E. did not like writing and thinking in woods (as I do), nor was he fond of mountains—he was ill at ease on mountains. What he preferred was a small bare eminence with a wide view—and this he got at Hawkes Point. "I take no man to a dinner-table, library, or exchange," said Walt Whitman, "but each man and each woman of you I

[1] Emerson.

lead upon a knoll." So with Havelock Ellis. Often when reading him I have thought—yes, he wrote that in the open air, not crunched over a desk in a study, but from a knoll opening upon a wide view of Nature with the roof of sky, the floor of flowers and sea. If one were asked to appraise his work with a single word, I suppose Harmony might do; but I would prefer Perspective. It is above all things perspective that we gain from reading him, and the calmness and hope inseparable from it, the capacity to sense the harmony, to reconcile the mighty opposites in creative conflict, to see the problem placed in the playground of Time.

When H.E. wrote his *Impressions and Comments* he gave an impression and he made a comment: that is, he held up an Image and he held up a Thought. A combination of the thing and the idea has always seemed to me the essence of the best descriptive writing. I do not doubt that he wrote the following in the open air, and it may well serve to illustrate with exactitude what I mean, to emphasize the felicity of precision in which he excelled, and to exemplify his power to raise our spirits by the lonely irony of the thought as native to one who kept watch upon eternity.

The wind has been blowing a stiff gale from the west all night and sudden squalls have swept in now and again. This morning the wind has dropped and the sky for a while is blue. But the sea is still alive; her pulse beats mightily from the sting of the wind's kisses. Her body is still restless and writhing, her limbs far flung. Not today, as so often, is she sending in the slow solemn ranks of rollers to curve smoothly and break delicately as they come to land. Today the waves rush in swiftly in great irregular masses, falling to pieces in their haste, to clash and melt in one another, or rise as they unite in a spasm of inverted cascades. Nearer in, the turbulent swift irregular waves crash wildly against the rocks in infinite variety of living motion, or roll back in some strangely irregular step of the dance-measure to leap into each other's arms, and then to bound on with renewed energy; and here mountains of foam arise as some huge boulder is struck; and here delicate whiffs ascend a few feet only, resting in the air long enough for the eye to catch the outline of their beauty; and here the foam mounts and spreads like a huge hand closing tenderly all over some slope of rock, inserting its fingers lovingly into every cranny. And now, as the tide sweeps nearer, the exuberant foam is everywhere leaping in great joyous white flames onto the cliffs, and again I see it surging up even beyond the dark high hill that shuts out the next inlet of the sea, even where the hill becomes a green slope, leaping in spires, amid vaster masses of foam, a cloudy exhilarating mist which floats softly towards me, while a low deep rumbling bass seems to furnish the pivot in which the wild fugal dance turns in harmonious rhythm.

So it is today. So it was in days long aeons before any of the things that we in our narrow sense call living moved on the earth. The waves clasped one another then with just as joyous love. There was life and there was play and there was art and there was music and dance. The same words would fit the waves then that we apply to our most admired beings of human flesh. But there was none to mark. So by some stress of unconscious desire Nature created her little mechanical living toys that could see and feel. It seemed not enough, so she created Man, who could not only see and feel but know, realizing the world from outside, as she realizes it, incorporating her Godhead of the Seventh Day. Therewith her desire was fulfilled and there was nothing more to do. Nature has had her whim. There was not so much in it after all. And she had to pay for it. Man proved a dangerous plaything. Only one problem remains: How to dispose of him?

She will solve the problem some day. On that day the sea will come rolling in with the same joyous life and the same bright beauty. But once a creature stood here who saw and felt and knew that beauty. It will have been enough.

H.E. was proud of the fact that he always kept an erect figure throughout life, on account of not writing over a desk (I say desk, by the way, as the conventional word, but no sane writer ever uses a desk, he uses a table)—and that people would remark that he had nothing of the appearance of the literary man. I'm not quite sure about this last: anyway, what

he looked like at this time, 1897, is seen by the photograph
taken in his study at Hawkes Point. He was then thirty-eight.
Edward Carpenter, in his delightful book, *My Days And
Dreams*, gives a few lines of description of H.E., though
what age he was referring to is uncertain. "The personality
of Havelock Ellis is that of a student, thoughtful, preoccupied, bookish, deliberate; yet unlike most students he has a
sort of grand air of Nature about him—a fine free head and
figure as of some great god Pan, with distant relations among
the Satyrs." Once when he and Olive Schreiner were in the
National Gallery together they stopped before Rubens's "Si-
lenus," and she drew attention to his resemblance to the satyr
on the right of the picture. I think Strobl's bust catches this
aspect—and gives us the man who wrote the books. Those
who made this observation also often observed his resemblance to Jesus Christ—as conceived in the imagination of
mankind. One day he was sitting on a bench awaiting a sur-
gical demonstration at St. Thomas's, when a student bent
over and said with a dry smile, "You remind me of Jesus
Christ." He frequently heard similar remarks in the following years. He himself comments upon this in his best natural
history manner, as if writing about someone else, and with
the same lofty indifference as to what the mob might think
as Whitman in his great poem "To Him That Was Crucified"
—"I do not think it was generally taken to be a resemblance
flagrantly in contrast with my satyr air. Nor would I myself see any contrast. Pan and the satyrs were divinities of
Nature, as was Jesus on another plane. The wild being of the
woods who knelt in adoration before the secret beauty of
sleeping nymphs was one at heart with the Prophet who
could see no more than a passing stain of sin in the wanton
woman kissing his feet." He confesses that as a boy he had a
horror of acquiring an artificially moulded and wrinkled face.
He tried to nip in the bud any wrinkling of forehead or con-
traction of lips. "This was by no means from fear of impair-
ing my good looks, for I never imagined I had any, but solely
because my natural and instinctive ideal involved a fluid re-

ceptivity of mind, an openness to impressions which was hostile to all rigidity and fossilized restraint, and I felt, doubtless rightly, that the hardening of mind and heart had its outward expression in a tightly contracted face."

I have mentioned at the beginning how in 1938 I got something of the impression of a sea-captain. The first time I saw him was in my twenties in the British Museum Reading Room. I made a notebook description. I am unwilling to quote much of it here since it is so difficult not to be irritated by the manner in which one wrote as a youth. I was carried away above all, it seems, by the sight of his hair: "It is so alive and smooth and silky, so healthy, so extraordinarily *thick*. I have never seen anything like it anywhere. Standing at one end of the Reading Room, I have seen it shine and glow at the other, or pass serenely along round the inner circle." I go on to say how I had never beheld such a god-like countenance, and then to give some details of how he stood. "I see him there by one of those standing desks at the side for resting heavy books taken directly from the shelves. I see him standing there with a volume on the desk. He is quite unconscious of all around, totally oblivious of everything but the matter in hand. Then he closes the book and goes to the shelf with it and takes another; but not as other men do these things; with a rhythm, a quiet sort of swing and roll which gives an impression of complete certainty and absolute self-unconsciousness. Again he stands by the desk with a new book. His clothes fit him exactly, seem beautiful and right: the brown shoes, strong wide brown tweed trousers, and grey-green light coat covering all loosely, everything *fitting*. The glorious hair, the nut-brown complexion, the beard, the superb forehead and shapely nose. He stands erect and still, absorbed. The great dome encircles the many readers, sitting and moving about. None notice him, a god in their midst; he notices none." The strongest impression which I carried away, and which has always remained with me, was his *absorption*, and the rhythmic, swinging gait. I thought there was something elephantine about the weight and at the same time delicacy of his motion, as index to the movements of his mind. He himself favoured comparison with the kangaroo. While in Australia he had been very taken with the way they would descend the hill slopes in large slow bounds, and later in life he wondered whether their appeal had not something to do with his own mental mode of progression. As for his absorption, his "self-unconsciousness" as I seem to have phrased it, this was central to him. He only saw what he wanted to see, and did not consider whether anyone saw him either. This trait was not entirely satisfactory for others. He admits: "Absorbed in my own dreams, all my life long I have passed by without seeing—and frequently, even when seeing, not recognizing—people who are perfectly well-known to me. I have even passed my own sweetheart who had come to seek me, and who let me pass, not revealing that incident to me until years afterwards."

12

THERE are few things of greater moment to a writer than *habitation*. H.E.'s good fortune in this respect was not confined to Hawkes Point at Carbis Bay. He had a foothold in London in one of the most enchanting places imaginable. He shared a flat at Fountain Court in the Temple with Arthur Symons, each with rooms completely independent of the other. Fountain Court lies between the river and Fleet Street. It used to be a favourite haunt of mine when I lived in London. You turned off from the noise and rumour of the Street, the Ministry of the Present Moment, into a sequestered pool of peace. True, these Temples in London are given over to Law. You do not enter into the atmosphere of a college quad nor of a cathedral cloister. But the effect is stronger because there is no expected atmosphere of learning or devotion; the quietness being set in the midst of unquiet thoughts and passing shows, works upon us the more powerfully. Before the Blitz, Fountain Court was the most appealing of these pockets; when you sat by the fountain you looked down upon a lawn and beyond to the Embankment which could be reached in a minute; and the Embankment at night, as H.E. said truly, presents a scene as lovely as can be found in any city in the world. In the evening the gates were closed as in a college, and sometimes on a summer evening H.E. and Symons would sit in the silent court beside the fountain, "now become as a Court of the Alhambra, marvellous in its deep peace only broken by the gentle plash of the water." H.E. did not possess a fortune: he possessed good fortune, which is better; and no millionaire could have improved his position with regard to habitation. He knew this, and it is not strange that just as he could never bear to revisit Hawkes Point after he had left it, so when in future years he passed the gates of this beloved spot he never felt able to enter the Court.

He shared the two compartments of the flat with Symons: he did not share his compartment with his wife. She made a point of not intruding upon him here. Fortressed in the Temple he might almost have been at Oxford in All-Souls which is designed for the promotion of bachelors. Indeed, at this time, and most of his life, he bore little of the stigmata of the married man. She was all for that, theoretically. Even so, H.E. never seems to have allowed enough for feminine inconsistency allied with protestations not consciously insincere, and in a curious letter actually wrote these words to her— "Louie and Symons came to the conclusion the other day that I had not been at all spoilt by marriage; you'd hardly know, Symons said to her, that I was married. Rhys, on the other hand, they decided, had been spoilt. Although better groomed than formerly (or perhaps because!) he looks pale and depressed, and has no spirit for anything; always has to be with his wife."

When staying at the Temple it was easy for him to go to the British Museum Reading Room, and do anything else he liked without much bother in travelling by bus or tube. And nearly every year he and Symons would go off together for some six weeks travelling abroad—journeys elaborately planned beforehand. In 1894 he went by himself to Rome under the auspices of the International Medical Congress, and was visited on his arrival by Lombroso, for his book *The Criminal* brought this invitation and thus he went free to the city he had most desired to see all his life, and he found that it surpassed his expectations. "It is only in Rome," he declared, "as I still continue to feel, that one realizes what it means to belong to the human species." It is not easy to see how he found the time or the money for his endless wanderings abroad, but I favour the view that he was a magician of some sort. I think he had a sleight of hand in relation to certain natural laws—notably the law of duration. However this may be, as the historians say, he wandered over much of Europe, including Russia, and this made it possible for him to write what he calls a fragment of his plan for a book on *The Genius of Europe*—which fragment is one of the most interesting of all his works.

A small particular example of the enrichment which his travels gave him can be found in *Affirmations*. It is clear that he had already been to Russia by the remarks he makes in his chapter on St. Francis when he contrasts the crowds he watched as a boy on Bank Holidays swarming round the Crystal Palace with the way the Russian crowds comport themselves on their festival days. I suppose that *Affirmations*, written in 1897, shares with *The Dance of Life* an equal recognition. Still, I can well imagine a normal, stiffish minded person, asking—Just what is he affirming? Unfortunately few writers ever existed who lend themselves less easily to the tabloid summary. And to say that he affirmed Life may leave those guessing who in their search for "a living" have forgotten the reasons for living. This is how he opens his chapter on St. Francis. It is rather a lengthy quotation, but I cannot bring myself to spoil it by cutting.

The religion of Jesus was the invention of a race which itself never accepted that religion. In the East religions spring up, for the most part, as naturally as flowers, and, like flowers, are scarcely a matter for furious propaganda. These deep sagacious Eastern men threw us of old this rejected flower, as they have since sent us the vases and fans they found too tawdry; and when we send our missionaries out to barter back the gift at a profit, they say no word, but their faces wear the mysterious Eastern smile. Yet for us, at all events, the figure of Jesus symbolizes, and will always symbolize, a special attitude towards life, made up of tender human sympathy and mystical reliance on the unseen forces of the world. In certain stories of the Gospels, certain sayings, in many of the parables, this attitude finds the completest expression of its sweetest abandonment. But to us, men of another race living in far distant corners of the world, it seems altogether oriental and ascetic, a morbid exceptional phenomenon. And as a matter of fact Jesus found no successor. Over the stage of those gracious and radiant scenes swiftly fell a fire-proof curtain, wrought of systematic theology and formal metaphysics, which even the divine flames of that wonderful personality were unable to melt.

Something even stronger than theology or metaphysics has served to cut us off from the spirit of Jesus, and that is the spirit of Paul, certainly the real founder of Christianity, as we know it, for Jerome, Augustine, Luther, were all the children of Paul, and in no respect the children of Jesus. That marvellous little Jew painted in its main outlines the picture of Christianity which in the theatre of this world has for so many centuries shut us off from Jesus. Impelled by the intense and concentrated energy of his twisted suffering nature, Paul brought "moral force" into our western world, and after it that infinite procession of hypocrisies and cruelties and artificialities which still trains loathsomely across the scene of civilized life. Jesus may have been a visionary, but his visions were in divine harmony with the course of nature, with the wine and the bread of life, with children and with flowers. We may be very sure that Paul never considered the lilies, or found benediction with children. He trampled on nature when it came in his way, and for the rest never saw it. He was not, as Festus thought, a madman, but whether or not, as his experiences seem to indicate, he was a victim to the "sacred disease" of epilepsy, concerning his profoundly neurotic temperament there can be no manner of question.

He flung himself onto men, this terrible apostle of the "Gentiles," thrusting faith down their throats at the point of a spiritual sword so fiery and keen that, by no miracle, it soon became a sword of steel with red blood dripping from its point. Wellnigh everything that has been evil in Christianity, its temporal power, its accursed intolerance, its contempt for reason, for beautiful living, for every sweet and sunny and simple aspect of the world —all that is involved in the awful conception of "moral force"— flows directly from Paul. What eternal torture could be adequate for so monstrous an offender? And yet, when you think of the potent personality concentrated in this morbid man, of his courage, of the intolerance that he wreaked on himself, the flashes of divine insight in his restless and turbulent spirit, of the humility of the neuropath who desired to be "altogether mad," the pathos of it all, indignation falls silent. What can be said?

We may note that the professional iconoclast or popular leader of thought seldom hits as hard as that. He has the box-office to consider. H.E. never thought of the box-office, or of fame, or of number of followers, or of interests and institutions arrayed against him. I have sometimes thought that the man who is not a satirist often makes most effect when satiric (viz., Carpenter's devastating *Desirable Mansions*), and that the merciful merciless thrust from him whose hand is seldom raised to strike plunges deepest. We live in a more whole-some age now—and H.E. may have had something to do with it. He was a nineteenth-century man, remember; Dr. Arnold had died young a few years before his birth, while Cardinal Manning was his contemporary for thirty-two years. We might well pause in contemplation before the terrible face that confronts us in the best known photograph of Manning, with the senseless severity and fear and disapproval in the eyes, and the ghastly tension of the lips drawn tight as by a bit in restraint of all the natural man within—a typical moral-force man, a specialist in thoughts about sin and sinfulness and the life-to-come and about what God was going to do with him when he died and so on. Or take Dr. Arnold—a real, first-class, Paul man. I note that even the warm admirers of Lytton Strachey, including Max Beerbohm, are inclined to rebuke him for his essay on Arnold as being in too much a vein of mockery. The assumption is that Dr. Arnold should not have been mocked. But how could any mockery be too much for such a man? The biographer knew what he was do-ing, what he was called upon to do. It is complained that he quoted things out of context and made them look bad. "It is very startling," said Arnold, looking round upon the boys at Rugby, "to see so much of sin combined with so little of sorrow." How do you make that remark look good?—and he did say it. He could not bear the fact that the naughtiest boys enjoyed themselves most. There were times when he nearly lost faith in his system of education, and began to wonder whether more radical reforms might not be necessary before the multitude of children under his charge "shouting and gambolling and yet plunged all the time deep in moral evil—could ever be transferred into a set of Christian gentlemen." In those days there were hundreds and hundreds of men like Arnold swarming like black beetles upon all that was innocent and natural and happy; and because of their moral force, and self-righteousness, and clarity of aim, and Church backing, and solemn fruity voices, they always got away with it and held positions of petty power. Yet in the simple eye of nature they were really monsters of depravity who made a mockery of Jesus Christ.

Since there is still cant and confusion upon issues of this sort, H.E. is scarcely out of date I fear, though he has dated passages. There is still nothing written today as clarifying and cleansing as this essay on St. Francis, the interpretation of sinner and saint in combination, of simplicity and of purity. His page is nearly always classic. Though he was, or gave the appearance of being, serene, he was passionate. But he held himself in check: all passion unspent: the emotion coiled up, hoarded, ready to spring, but kept in place. Yet sometimes he nearly spilt, though never spoilt, the passion. This piece on St. Francis rises almost into a hymn of joy, an ecstasy of affirmation. I am sure he wrote it in the open air at Hawkes Point. He saw all that was essential for living, all that could be cast aside, all the simple joy that is for ever open to mankind. He was lifted up in spirit as one who might have cried from his high place—Come unto me all ye who are weary and heavy laden with false values, false sense of sin, false negativities foisted on you by the righteous; be yourselves; be emerald; fear not; and thus shall you enter into Paradise, for Paradise is here.

In the same book he wrote about Nietzsche, Casanova,

Huysmans, and Zola in order to make further affirmations. The choice was quite arbitrary, but he was not without his own brand of vanity, and he chose to write about men unknown (and untranslated) in England at that time. Indeed it is only very recently that Casanova and Huysmans have come into fashion. Nietzsche's reputation has gone up and down according to the fashionable line of approach. H.E. was not concerned with the superman, master-moralist chunk which engages the assault of the anti-Nietzschean and the approval of the Nietzschean. It was his lyrically affirmative attitude towards life which appealed to H.E., his view, that life being so multi-form and many-coloured, each man should have the courage to be himself—which would include being his own moralist and his own philosopher. Here is Life, a dazzling wealth of types, forms, avenues, approaches. Yet up comes the moralist saying—No, you musn't do *this*, you must listen to me and do *that*. You have no right to *your* categorical imperative, you must follow *mine*. H.E. held, with Nietzsche and Ibsen and many others, that we should each work it out for ourselves as we go along, as an art, the art of life. Of course it is a council of perfection, and only for the strong. The art of the weak must always be glad submission to the dictates of others. The free approach must seem too dangerous; to your Tom, Dick, and Harry, to your churchman, your alderman, your lord mayor, your Member of Parliament, it simply spells anarchy. But it does not spell anarchy. Not even for the weak man. Everyone who is not absolutely blinded by self-deception knows that nearly every hour of every day, in the home, in the street, in the shop, in the office, we make our morality as we go along, as an art, according to our strength in the art of living, relying upon Nature, upon our innate sense of decency. The man who does not do this frequently drives his wife mad, and his children mad: most women do it as a matter of course. As for the men who preach the golden rule that there is no golden rule, they are nearly always the self-disciplinarians, the non-self-indulgers, and it was Nietzsche who said that "every day is badly spent in which a man has not once denied himself." This matter is both simple and subtle at the same time (as are most fundamentals); if we cannot be simple and subtle simultaneously, we can scarcely make this approach. We have to face inconsistency in behaviour, perhaps also in thought, for I am well aware that H.E. and the others are themselves proposing a principle, preaching a moral. But at least they do not enunciate a string of negatives. They believed that if we devote ourselves to the things that are good to do we need trouble ourselves little about the things that are good to leave undone.

It was a typical piece of audacity that H.E. should have brought Casanova into this book of affirmations. No doubt there is a touch of bravado in it. But I think he carries it off, even while admitting that Casanova might technically be regarded as a moral imbecile. He saw him as a magnificent piece of natural machinery; certainly not a pillar of society nor a knocker-down of the pillars of society, but one who took the world as it is and himself as he was, and set forth the whole of himself without disguise. It would be a poor picture of the world which would show us a St. Bernard or a Spinoza or a Leonardo da Vinci and shut out a Casanova, and thus deny ourselves the spectacle of the human animal in the completest development of his rankness and cunning and wit.

It is not my aim to be exhaustive in speaking of any book, merely to give one man's view of Havelock Ellis and his works—it would be folly to attempt more in so wide a field. Thus—one more remark only about *Affirmations*. H.E. was fifty years in advance when he wrote about Huysmans. To-day he is not unfamiliar to us in England, and 1956 saw the publication of Mr. James Laver's searching study. I do not know that H.E.'s essay preaches any very clear gospel, but one thing has so stuck in my mind that I think I should include it as a conclusion. How get the devil to flee? By determination? by teeth-setting resolution? by taking a firm disciplinarian grip on oneself? No, said Huysmans, that's not the best way of dealing with the Evil One. There is only one sure way—*let drop.* "There are two ways of ridding ourselves of a thing which burdens us, casting it away or letting fall. To cast away requires an effort of which we may not be capable, to let fall imposes no labour, is simpler, without peril, within reach of all. To cast away, again, implies a certain interest, a certain animation, even a certain fear; to let fall is absolute indifference, absolute contempt; believe me, use this method, and Satan will flee."

13

—————

HE HAD already written in "The Contemporary Science Series," and published in 1894, *Man and Woman*, which was meant as his prolegomena towards the *Studies in the Psychology of Sex*. Even so it is well worth reading on its own account, and it is not surprising that by 1904 it was in its fourth edition, and was translated into many languages. It provides a good second example of his inherent anthropological, natural-historian approach to the realities of life. "To me the tragedy and comedy of life lie in the consequences, sometimes terrible, sometimes ludicrous, of our persistent attempts to found our institutions on the ideals suggested to our imaginations by our half-satisfied passions, instead of on a genuinely scientific *natural history*" (my emphasis). Those words, it will be remembered, were written by Bernard Shaw in his Preface to *Plays Pleasant*. His attitude to life was also that of the natural historian, not of the idealist or the moralist. He never wavered in it, and he was not false to it in life: thus, for example, when many other literary men had deserted Oscar Wilde in his trouble, he remained helpful and loyal to that unfortunate genius to the end. Shaw would have appreciated a remark which an American scientist made to H.E., to the effect that he used the facts of social behaviour as facts of natural history to be discussed as any other biological facts. Now, before we can get our psychology right, and before we can give rein to ideals, we should get our physiology right. *Man and Woman* might have been called "The Physiology of the Sexes," since the psychology rises so much from the physiology. The same might be said of his famous *Studies*, and I have always wondered why he called them the *Psychology* of Sex since he deploys so much physiology as the basis of the whole thing. We all realize this basis in a vague and dim way, noting for example how the blood leaves a man's face and he turns white when very afraid—a remarkable sight. But perhaps few of us carry our apprehension far enough to realize the extent of the welding between emotion and motion. It had been supposed, before this kind of investigation had been introduced by H.E., that emotion is a purely mental phenomenon and that love and anger, for instance, could go on in the brain in the same way as an arithmetical calculation. Yet this is not so. The emotions of anger or fear or love are bound up with the vascular and muscular systems. "Just as it may be said: no muscle, no motion; so it may equally be said: no muscle, no emotion."

Man and Woman goes thoroughly into the physiological differences between men and women and classifies the characteristics of the male and female form: the growth and proportions of the body, the evolution of the pelvis in relation to the evolution of the sexual emotion, the skull and the brain; the senses—touch, sensibility to pain, smell, taste, hearing, sight, coloured hearing; muscular strength; metabolism —of the blood, respiration, excretion, susceptibility to poisons, hair and pigmentation; the viscera—the thyroid gland, the voice, the stomach and its allies; the functional periodicity of women. Thus when we ask a leading question: Why is a woman a woman? there is no call to be vague; we say that she is a woman because of her internal secretions, and that a man is a man by the totality of his internal secretions— though the study of these facts brings the realization that few women are all woman and few men are all man.

If we pay due heed to the basic facts we shall expect inclination and behaviour to be in harmony with those facts.

In a broad way we do expect this: we know for instance that the constitution of women is unlikely to make them keen to take up engineering. We recognize that in so far as the main production of women is the production of mankind they are clearly more at home in the home than men, just as we recognize that the constitution of men unfits them to deal with children. All this is obvious, and it ought to be obvious that any claim to "superiority" on either side has nature against it, since such a lop-sided race could scarcely continue to exist (difficult as it must be for any woman with a baby not to feel superior to men). But our understanding is not carried far enough. Thus, the caution and indirectness of women, the habit of getting what they want by ruses, are so marked that Lombroso declared that in women deception is "almost physiological." It should be clear that this has nothing to do with innate wickedness; it is inevitable and results from the constitution of women which provides them with weaker muscles, for one thing, than men. Again, I myself have been accustomed to point out, too complacently, the fact that we may search through history without finding a single woman philosopher of any note; but H.E., while giving further evidence in support of this assertion, points out that this is because the whole bent of women is for the concrete and away from the abstract, which is part and parcel of their capacity to hold the world together while men create the conditions of the world. And since women are intelligent rather than intellectual they do not in the least mind this view. The contribution of both sides is so equal that there should not be the slightest need for either to make false claims. Thus for every one man who is an artist in living there are about twenty women. Men should not gibe at this since they are artists in other forms than that of life. But men do not accept this easily, while on the other hand we hear the claim made over and over again by women that the reason why they have seldom attained eminence in any of the fine arts—with the exception of some novel-writing, and of acting, where they are largely superior to men—is because they have hitherto not had the opportunity, and we can hope for great things in the future. Yet the truth is that when they *have* attained eminence they have done so exactly as men have done it—by overcoming, and indeed building upon, obstacles and difficulties at every turn.

H.E. calls *Man and Woman* a "little book," yet it contains over five hundred and fifty pages which embrace not only the physiological facts but the psychology arising out of them, and included a sensational chapter on "Hypnotic Phenomena." This was certainly a book which he could not have written without his medical training, and he could draw upon the facts he had been obliged to learn for his anatomical examinations. It is a volume which cannot fail to widen the outlook of everyone willing to understand the respective functions of Man and Woman. H.E. has been regarded as the greatest champion of women which the age of such champions produced, and if today we hear much less about their "rights" it is because so many of those rights have been won. I do not think there is any need nowadays for a man to describe himself as a feminist: it is as unnecessary, and as silly, as for a woman to describe herself as a masculinist.

14

THE ground had now been cleared for the study of sex in the central sense in which he was chiefly concerned with it. The time had come for him to publish his first volume. But everything went wrong.

It happened that this first volume was on homosexuality. He had not originally planned to start with that aspect of his subject, but various reasons and circumstances combined to make *Sexual Inversion* his starting point. When it was completed he set to work to find a publisher. A friend told him of an excellent man of some wealth who was about to set up a publishing house for the purpose of unostentatiously printing scientific and philosophic works unlikely to appeal to the larger public—just the sort of man H.E. wanted. This man's name was Astor Singer, his London agent being Dr. Roland de Villiers. H.E. paid the latter a visit, and arranged with him for the publication of this first volume on a financial basis which seemed satisfactory. All appeared to be well. But very soon it became plain that there was something shady about Roland de Villiers. The name of his firm was first given as suggesting connection with a famous publishing house, then suddenly changed to The Watford University Press, though no university had the smallest association with it. The colleague of de Villiers, Astor Singer, was always off stage either at the Riviera or in Mexico; in fact he never achieved visibility for the reason that he existed only in the imagination of de Villiers who nevertheless spoke of him with ever increasing respect and awe. "Mrs. Singer" was discovered to be living in de Villiers's house and eventually turned out to be his wife, and it was now learnt that de Villiers was not his real name. This was Georg Ferdinand Springmuhl von Weissenfeld, a well educated German who had obtained honours in science, medicine, and literature, had married into a good family, had become estranged from his father, and after forging some cheques had fled to England in 1880 where he soon found himself sentenced to a year's imprisonment for forgery and other offences. He had a passion for mystification and fraud. He invented so many characters for himself that in order to avoid confusion he was obliged to keep a register in which he entered each alias with its specific signature. He established a Brandy Distillery Company Ltd. which consisted of himself alone, and circulated a prospectus containing photographs of its vineyards that did not exist, thereby securing a capital of £60,000 which made it advisable for him to have thirty distinct banking accounts in London under different names. He enlisted servants to aid his mystifications so that when he held a reception his housemaids, cooks, and nurses, elaborately dressed for the part, would be introduced to the distinguished guests as the wives and daughters of statesmen, ambassadors, scientists, and artists. But if any suspicious person called upon him unexpectedly he was not easily found, for he was an adept in secret passages, concealed cupboards, and disguised exits. Add to this reports of unscrupulous sexual depravity, and it will scarcely seem surprising that the police later declared him to be one of the most interesting criminals of modern times.

Such was the man whom H.E. had selected as the publisher for the first volume of the *Studies*. Yet de Villiers did carry out his obligations and print the book, and even paid the author the agreed advance. It was sent to a few medical and scientific journals in which it was reviewed in a respectful and appreciative tone.

Then the drama began. It was not caused by any unprofessional behaviour on the part of de Villiers, though it was fully in accord and indeed perfectly congruous with the general conduct of his affairs. *Sexual Inversion* became involved with a Society of the day called The Legitimation League. It was a little society which held advanced views on marriage and parenthood, sought to promote the legitimization of illegitimate children, and published an organ, entitled *The Adult*, edited by a man called George Bedborough who goes down to history on account of Havelock Ellis. For though H.E. had no connection with the League or *The Adult* it turned out that de Villiers was in touch with Bedborough and got him to stock a few copies of *Sexual Inversion* at the offices of the League. Now it generally happens that this sort of Society is inclined to attract people who have nothing to do with its main motive; and so it came about that some anarchists appeared at meetings of the League regardless of the fact that anarchism played no part in its aims. Since there was a special "anarchist section" at Scotland Yard, whose job it was to take care of anarchists, the attention of the police was directed to The Legitimation League on the premises of which they discovered *Sexual Inversion*, and it seemed to them that they could crush the League (identified with anarchism) by exposing the book as an immoral document. A police spy attended the meetings, won the confidence of Bedborough, and gathered sufficient data to bring a case against him. Thus on May 31st, after a copy of the book had been purchased, Bedborough was arrested. H.E. heard the news in Cornwall from de Villiers who, true to form, added that he had been privately informed that H.E. was also to be arrested. De Villiers himself thought it best to disappear "to Cologne" (though he may not have left his house), but not before authorizing H.E. to undertake legal representation for which he would pay expenses. And he did pay: for it should be added here that de Villiers was never regarded by H.E. as falling within the category of "criminal," but rather as a special though unspecified psychological case of what might be fairly called mystificationmania. Personally I think he was just crooked; and it is notable that your crook will on occasion be straight with one person just as a mean man will sometimes be consecutively generous with one person whom he respects.

H.E. went up to London to make arrangements for the defence of his book, the League looking after the defence of Bedborough. Edith at this moment was in Manchester with Claire, and he wrote at once to tell her the news. Instantly she was at his side, cheerful, helpful, combative—his *support*. This is when true love is revealed—to be treasured even by us who having some share in him have yet no share in her. "None was ever more staunch in emergencies, so prompt, so resourceful, so consoling," he says. "She whose physical temperament made her apt to fall into nervous terrors over mere nothings, whose health was always uncertain, who had just been told that the condition of her heart was worse and that she must avoid all worry, simply and as a matter of course flung all such considerations aside when a real trouble faced one whom she loved, and revealed, as Froissart said of the Countess of Montfort, the heart of a lion."

The case dragged on for six months. It was not dramatic— just a muddle. The counts of Regina v. Bedborough were unconnected. One was that Bedborough had "sold and uttered a certain lewd wicked bawdy scandalous and obscene libel in the form of a book entitled *Studies in the Psychology of Sex: Sexual Inversion.*" Other counts dealt with publications of the League. It would have been possible to uphold the book and disapprove of the League's publications, or vice versa— but the issue was confused since there was no connection between the two things. Though leading authorities in the medico-psychological world paid H.E. handsome testimonials, none of them were prepared to go into the witness box in his defence. H.E. would not go himself, since he had no authoritative ground to stand on, and he also felt that his weakness in the way of giving any sort of public performance such as making a speech, would cause him to be a bad witness. Thus, though a great number of brilliant and prominent people (including Bernard Shaw) set up a Free Press Defence Committee, nothing effective could be done since all the doctors and official men declined to be drawn in. Nevertheless great hopes were rested on counsel for the defence who had been selected with care—a Mr. Avory who was later to be known as one of the ablest lawyers of his generation. He was looking out for a chance to distinguish himself and would unquestionably have made a splendid case. But Bedborough's solicitor had not been chosen carefully. He was a limp, shabby, shady, and indeed shocking person who, after a great deal of doing worse than nothing, apppropriated the £200 set aside as fee for Counsel, and according to etiquette it was impossible for Avory to appear. Bedborough was not represented, the book not defended, the case was lost, and the Judge addressed the following words to the defendant: "You might at the outset perhaps have been gulled into the belief that someone might say that this is a scientific book. But it is impossible for anyone with a head on his shoulders to open the book without seeing that it is a pretence and a sham, and that it is merely entered into for the purpose of selling this filthy publication." So much for the Law. Could the journalists be far behind? H.W. Massingham, at that time editor of *The Daily Chronicle*, had shown sympathy towards the case, and H.E. hastened from the Court to his office, but Massingham refused to see him, being too much impressed by the weighty and searching remarks of the judge, and in writing about that judgment now expressed his opinion that the book was scientifically valueless, and in the "discharge of his duty to the public" felt constrained to say that the book should never have been printed, being not only morbid but "worthless as science." Thus the Law and the Press tried to dismiss him and his book from the world. They could not do so. They had not the force to do so. It was Havelock Ellis who held the reins of power. They thought they had dismissed him from the world. "Yet I—rather the spirit of man I chanced to embody—have overcome the world. My "filthy" and "worthless" and "morbid" book has been translated into all the great living languages to reach people who could not say what a Recorder is, nor read *The Daily Chronicle* even if they ever saw it." Thus, as so often happens, the calamity was not really a calamity but a piece of good fortune. The trial, though a ghastly thing for such a man to endure, saved him from being published by a scoundrel.

Rather symbolically perhaps, when the show was over the puppets almost immediately fell to pieces. The judge died so soon afterwards that many people thought that he must have been struck to the heart by the things that were said to him about his part in the trial. Others connected with it swiftly followed him into oblivion, and finally the police caught up with de Villiers. Having established his identity and worked out his history they called on his home at Cambridge where he was living under another name. On perceiving their approach he made use of his elaborate escape system. But the police were not to be balked and at last a secret panel was discovered leading to a passage where the haggard de Villiers was found with a revolver which was then struck from his hand. He was brought out handcuffed. But he was still resourceful. With a great show of agitation he called for a glass of water, sipped it, and fell dead. He had been wearing a ring, behind the seal of which he had once boasted that there was a poison that would instantly kill a man.

H.E. was now free to start again, though steadfastly determined not to publish in England—a resolve from which he never wavered. He offered his work to America, and, without delay, the F.A. Davis Company agreed to publish the book, not now as the first in the Series, but as the second volume—the first being *The Evolution of Modesty*, which he had ready, and it still remains the first of the seven volumes.

He had modestly chosen to issue his work in the quietest and most unobtrusive way he could manage, almost privately. But that force which fights against knowledge and liberation in the name of order and respectability, killed, not the book, but the method of publication. Instead of a few copies being sold by an obscure firm, the *Studies* went to an active medical publishing house in America with a high reputation and a staff of experienced travellers. By his proposed method which was closed to him by the court, his books would perhaps have sold by the dozen; but "by the method Order and Respectability compelled me to adopt," he declares, "they have sold, and continue today to sell steadily, on a far larger scale, in an ever increasing circle round the world." It was not the first nor the last time that the New World had come to redress the balance of the Old.

H.E. always held that science had begun at the wrong end. It began with the stars and not for a long time did it work its way towards man himself. In his Dialogue about the Nineteenth Century there is a passage on the curious fact that great expensive observatories were built for the minute study of the stars while it was yet considered almost morally wrong to study the laws of human life. "They knew all about the laws of what they called gravitation, but they thought it impure to ascertain the laws by which human beings are attracted to one another and repelled." If only science could have started from the right end we might be in better shape today, he felt.

It was this which he sought to remedy in his seven volumes on the Psychology of Sex. "Now that the problem of religion has been practically settled," he said, in his characteristic manner, "and that the problem of labour has at least been placed on a practical foundation, the question of sex stands before us as the chief problem." He did not hope to solve it, but he felt that if he could succeed in stating it we would have at least half of knowledge. For the trouble about ignorance here is that it leads to the attempt to suppress what cannot be suppressed, but can be perverted. In other civilizations the sexual instinct could often grow up and develop wholesomely. In our modern civilization we do not allow it to develop wholesomely. H.E. mentions the creditable attempt of the Catholic Church to ventilate the subject in the *De Matrimonio* of Sanchez. In this the sexual life of man was set out in an admirable spirit of objectivity and even scientific accuracy. But it was paraded in its relationship to sin: we learn what is a lawful sin, and what is a mortal sin. But today we need the same spirit and temper applied from a different standpoint. Now we want to know what is normal and abnormal in relation to physiology and psychology. We want to know what is lawful to man as a child of Nature rather than as a child of sin. We want to know what is a venial sin against Nature, and what is a mortal sin against Nature—though this sort of ruling was easier for the theologians.

It may surprise some readers—as it certainly surprised me until I examined what was in the books—that seven volumes calling for half a life-time's labour would be necessary on this theme. It may seem a curious comment upon modern civilization. I think it is. And no one who is not a psychiatrist or doctor can possibly feel called upon to read all the books. But the genuine scientist and investigator does his job thoroughly: he ventilates the subject in all its aspects, he covers the whole ground. Then whatever aspect is a problem to any given person can be studied in these pages coolly set forth in the manner of a natural historian, and, as it happens here and is unlikely ever to happen again, by an artist in words. Thus, to take a single example, and the most obvious of all, auto-erotism, there is not one of us, male or female, who would not profit by getting the facts straight about this in our youth.

In writing this book on Havelock Ellis it was never my intention to dwell upon his famous *Studies*, simply because they are famous and acknowledged throughout the world. They need no recommendation from me and it is not a field in which I can comment fruitfully. I merely pause to pay tribute to the titanic task. At the same time it occurs to me that some readers may wish to know just what the volumes consist of. I am willing to indicate this briefly.

Volume I deals with *The Evolution of Modesty, The*

Phenomenon of Sexual Periodicity, and Auto-Erotism. He opens a window onto a wide field in relation to modesty; its different aspects according to race and era; its base of fear in children and animals; its place in courtship as a necessary foundation for audacities. We are then shown how important it is to grasp the fact of sexual periodicity, so that men can understand the deep-rooted phenomenon of women's menstruation and all that it implies, and women the cycles in men; and it is pointed out that just as there is a seasonal periodicity in rapes and outbreaks among prisoners and a seasonal curve in suicide and insanity, so in earlier times the annual sexual rhythm, being less inhibited and thus more obviously pronounced, compelled the Church to license seasonal erotic orgies and festivals such as the Feast of Fools. Finally, in this volume, we come to auto-erotism and learn how much more this field covers than masturbation, a vast area of normal life more or less infused by auto-erotic phenomena. This chapter, going so fully into the subject, has brought enlightenment and liberation to the guilt-darkened victims of the nineteenth century. Regarding Freud's over-well known idea that everything could be traced to sex, it might be useful to give the view of Havelock Ellis: "The sexual impulse is not, as some have imagined, the sole root of the most massive human emotions, the most brilliant human aptitudes—of sympathy, of art, of religion. In the complex human organism, where all the parts are so many-fibred and so closely interwoven, no great manifestation can be reduced to a single source. But it largely enters into and moulds all these emotions and aptitudes, and that by virtue of its two most peculiar characteristics: it is, in the first place, the deepest and most volcanic of human impulses, and, in the second place—unlike the only other human impulse with which it can be compared, the nutritive impulse—it can to a large extent be transmuted into a new force capable of the strangest and most various uses."

Volume II—that is, the Volume I of the Bedborough Trial—deals, as we know, with *Sexual Inversion.* This means the sexual instinct turned by inborn constitutional abnormality towards persons of the same sex—in some cases turned so strongly that H.E. is able to quote a woman as declaring, "I cannot conceive a sadder fate than to be a woman—an average woman reduced to the necessity of loving a man!" In this volume H.E. gives a formidable historical survey of men and women who have been inverts, many of them being persons of exceptional intellect and high character and moral leadership; and it is a survey which also includes homosexuality among birds, dogs, rams, bulls, white rats, cockchafers, monkeys, and pigeons. He devotes chapters exclusively to the authorities on the subject; to the theory of it, the treatment of it, and the attitude of society to it (in many cases what worries the invert is not conscience nor police but the attitude of the world). In most of his volumes he includes fascinating case histories and appendices, and here we have accounts of "Homosexuality Among Tramps" and "The School Friendship of Girls." It is unquestionably one of the most important of these *Studies*, and after fifty years has already begun to effect legislation.

The third volume is called *The Analysis of the Sexual Impulse, Love and Pain, The Sexual Impulse in Women*. In this he deals with some of the most essential fundamental problems. Analysis is called for, he insists, for "unless we understand the exact process which is being worked out beneath the shifting and multifold phenomena presented to us we can never hope to grasp in their true relations any of the normal or abnormal manifestations of this instinct." In his study of Love and Pain he discusses the sources of those aberrations which are called sadism and masochism, aspects often expressed in the impulse to strangle, the desire to whip or be whipped, not to mention biting. He points out how Pain and not Cruelty is the essential element in sadism and masochism, and how these desires (and actions) are linked with normal and fundamental aspects of the sex impulse, and in elementary forms are found to be normal and in some degree present at some point in sex development—for their threads are subtly woven in and out of the whole psychological process of sex and not easily reduced to simplicity. Finally, while the sexual impulse in men is fairly obvious and well understood, he shows how in women it is even more important and a good deal more obscure in terms of qualitative difference.

Since love, seen in the broad biological aspect, is only in a limited extent a response to beauty, H.E. makes clear in Volume IV that to a greater extent beauty is simply a name for the complex of stimuli which most adequately arouses love—through touch, smell, hearing, and, above all, vision. Thus in Volume IV, called *Sexual Selection in Man* he examines this aspect of his Study and goes into its many ramifications, exploring the significance of the skin as the mother of all the senses; the place of the bath and the history of cleanliness; the origins of the kiss, its relation to biting, and its expression even among snails, birds, and dogs; the story of sound, including that of the voice, in the rhythm of sexual selection; the primitiveness of smell, the differentiation of odours, the influence of perfumes; and the primacy of vision in all this machinery through the appeal of beauty, the allure of adornment, the attraction of stature, the use of mirrors in feeding the lust of the eyes, and the magnetism of movement in the mystery of the dance.

Volume V treats of *Erotic Symbolism, The Mechanism of Detumescence, The Psychic State of Pregnancy.* In the first he reveals how sexual symbolism gives us the key that makes perversions intelligible; in the second he carefully and fully studies "the one physiological act in which two individuals are lifted out of all ends that centre in self and become the instrument of those higher forces which fashion the species; and in the third he comes to the psychic state of the woman who thus occupies the supreme position when she can perform the everlasting miracle which all the romance of love and all the cunning devices of tumescence and detumescence have been invented to make manifest.

Lastly in Volume VI—for I do not consider it necessary

to summarize Volume VII with *Eonism and other Supplementary Studies*—we come to *Sex in Relation to Society*. It is a very long book. It has been read more, I think, than the other studies, for its matter is of such universal importance and interest. It deals with the mother and her child; with sexual education and with nakedness; with the valuation of purely sexual love; with the function of chastity; with the problem of sexual abstinence; with prostitution; with the conquest of the venereal diseases; with sexual morality; with marriage; with the art of love; and with the science of procreation. I content myself with a list. I close with what are almost his own closing words. "We have now at last reached the point from which we started, the moment of conception, and the child again lies in its mother's womb. There remains no more to be said. The divine cycle is completed."

On the 7th of August, 1909, he wrote in his pocket diary— the only entry, he says, which was not a series of bald statements—these words: "The work that I was born to do is done." In his Autobiography he describes the sense of serene exultation which he then experienced. There had been fifteen years of preparation, and fifteen years of execution: while during all the time he noted and stored up every fact that came along bearing upon his theme, so that a vast amount of miscellaneous material from many sources was ready to his hand. It gives the impression of immense encyclopaedic erudition. This annoyed him. He wanted to be praised, not for the accumulation of facts, but for the artistic skill with which he had given them shape. This is always the artist's plea: Do not praise me for what I have said, but for how I have said it. After all, it matters little what a man says if he does not know how to say it—for otherwise it can have no effect, it cannot last, it will perish. Technique is genius. We can all be inspired. We can all be intoxicated by Beauty and the Voice of God. We can all amass mountains of information. But to give shape to these things, to give them a significant form—for this we need the tools of the artist, the hardness of his hammer and the heat of his fire. He comes before us in two ways. He may make much out of almost nothing: a stray remark, a swift glance from the window at something in the street may give him all he needs—with a few chance boughs and scattered stones he builds his house. That has always been one of the privileges of the artist, held before us in that parable which tells how once a supreme Artist with no more than two loaves and three fishes could yet feed five thousand men, or, with the same ease, turn water into wine. That is one mode in which the artist moves. And there is that other mode, when he gathers in and gathers up material from all the corners of the earth, and delves into the dust of great libraries to pick out as with a pincers the thing he needs. In this we know how marvellously Gibbon succeeded in his *Decline:* and we know how signally Spengler failed in his—not to mention the Teutonic books on Sex! I do not claim, and H.E. was far from claiming, that in the *Studies* he had created a great work of art. Yet art is there—with its property to effect and to endure. And it is assuredly there in this, the further function of the artist, that of enlarging our sphere of vision by bringing light into the places of darkness and revaluing the world's good, "ever choosing the base and despised things of the world, even the things that are not, to put to nought the things that are." [1] It had always been the instinct of H.E. "to spiritualize the things that have been counted low and material, if not disgusting," and at the last he had earned the right to say "where others have seen all things secular I have seen all things sacred."

Yet a question remains—however much it may surprise, coming from me now. *Was it worth it?* I have high hopes in being able to answer this question, but feel bound to raise it if only because it has often occurred to me. Here was no specialist in sex, let alone a sex genius in life. Here was a man who has often been acclaimed as the greatest critic of his age in the literary and philosophic and religious field, one of the greatest and most wide-ranging minds of all time. Was it a

[1] *Affirmations,* on Huysmans.

good thing for him to spend thirty years on studying sex so elaborately that this work stood between him and his other work of salvation? Was there any point in being so minute, so detailed in the research, investigating, for example, the mysteries pertaining to scatologic symbolism, urolagnia, corprolagnia, shoe-fetishism, and the future of the little toe? And again, was it worth it if, in spite of the fame of the *Studies* they can be obtained only in about two libraries and if one hardly ever meets anyone who has read them, whether layman or doctor? Perhaps these are fair questions. I would meet them as follows. One: he felt *called* to do this. That is good enough for me when the man thus called was so balanced. Two: it is perfectly true that science started at the wrong end: we have not made the stars any happier by investigating them first, while we could have made ourselves happier by self-knowledge. Here was a task that had to be done: the setting down of the physiological and psychological facts concerning that instinct in mankind which produces mankind. Three: if such an undertaking is to be carried out it must be done thoroughly in a professional comprehensive scientific manner: the whole terrain must be covered. This Havelock Ellis accomplished. Four: while claiming artistic skill and critical judgment in using the material, though disclaiming that he had created a great work of art, he adds—"I had done mankind a service which mankind needed, and which, it seemed, I alone was fitted to do. I had helped to make the world, and to make the world in the only way that it can be made, the interior way, by liberating the human spirit. The gratitude of men and women has made me humble." Now that is true. He did liberate the human spirit just as Freud did in his field. If to the pure all things are pure, it is also a fact that to the impure all things are impure. H.E. restored the meaning of Purity. "It would need a history of English morals," wrote my friend, Sir Russell Brain, "to explain the nuances of the word 'purity,' but it is significant that a word which in the first instance implies freedom from alien elements should have come to mean freedom from sexual feelings produced by repression and extolled as a virtue. If today the word 'purity' in this sense is hardly heard outside certain religious circles and even there induces a slightly uncomfortable self-consciousness we owe it to Havelock Ellis more than to anyone else. And yet if the word could be rehabilitated there is no one to whom it could be applied more aptly. He was a new type of man, one of the first in our era to view sex without the emotion of guilt. He was free from alien elements because to him there were none. We who come after him are fortunate that his gift as an artist enabled him to emancipate others as well as himself." [1] It is immaterial now whether the books are read. They are known to be there. That is enough. The monster is slain. The air has been cleaned. The stone has been rolled from the mouth of the cave. And the result is that we live in a different climate of thought about all this than before the coming of the liberator. All these things can henceforth be publicly discussed and worked out, and we are free from it all and can go forward to solve the remaining problems of life. Havelock Ellis was necessary, though if he had not existed it would have been optimistic to try and invent him.

[1] *Eugenics Review*, 1939.

15

A FEW weeks after the Bedborough Trial, when he had fixed up with his American publisher and finished Volume II of the Series, to be published as Volume I, he and his wife left England for a needed change of atmosphere, and went to Tangier and Malaga, and having completely recuperated after some of the most delightful experiences in their lives, returned to Cornwall.

In the highest spirits he sat down in his boat-summerhouse at Hawkes Point and wrote the ironic and exuberant short book, *The Nineteenth Century: A Dialogue in Utopia*. It has always been one of my favourites. He says that he wrote it swiftly and without premeditation as a sudden reaction to the then current eulogies of the nineteenth century. I have never taken easily to Utopia books, though their evolution during the last hundred years is enlightening, since we have witnessed a turning from an excess of optimism to an excess of pessimism. Nothing seems quite so strange to us today as the boundless optimism of the early meliorists in the nineteenth century. "Universal suffrage will at once change the whole character of society," said a Chartist leader. "From a state of watchfulness, doubt, and suspicion it will change to that of brotherly love, reciprocal interest, and universal confidence." The leader Benbow declared that in two days the working classes would be free. Fergus O'Connor went further. "Six months after the Charter is passed," he declared, "every man, woman, and child in the country will be well fed, well housed, and well clothed," and he was good enough to name the 29th of September, 1839, as the date fixed for the coming of the millennium. Still, by 1890, William Morris was in high hopes. In his *News From Nowhere* he also gives the date when everything will be all right—namely, in 1962. In his Utopia mechanism has disappeared (as it had also disappeared from Butler's *Nowhere*, though in neither case are we told how); everyone is good-looking and happy; all that is bad in human nature has been eliminated, all that is good retained. It is not surprising that Huxley was soon to arrive with his *Brave New World*, followed by Orwell who, in his *Nineteen Eighty-Four*, was also kind enough to give us the date when everything would be all wrong, exhibiting a world in which all that is good in human nature has been eliminated, all that is bad retained.

H.E., writing in 1900, did not fall into either of these excesses. He does not give us a Nowhere at all. Two men, belonging to a very far distant future, talk about the nineteenth century. He does not make the slightest attempt to give personality to these two men and therefore we do not complain that they are merely mouthpieces since they are meant to be merely mouthpieces. From that vantage point the century can be looked at as from a great height and seen in the perspective of ages. Morris also used his puppets to look back on the century and ventilate his views. That is the good part of the book, while the other part is no more nourishing to the mind than a dish of turkish delight is to the body. Certainly Morris and H.E. share equal honours on the theme of colonization. Let us note in passing that both these men were wholly English. No nation has praised itself so much and in so many ways as the English—none has blamed itself more. Here is William Morris:

The appetite of the World-Market grew with what it fed on: the countries within the ring of civilization (that is, organized misery) were glutted with the abortions of the market, and force and fraud were used unsparingly to open up countries *outside* that pale. This process of opening up is a strange one to those who have read the professions of the men of that period and do not understand their practice; and perhaps shows us at its worst the great vice of the nineteenth century, the use of hypocrisy and cant to evade the responsibility of vicarious ferocity. When the civilized World-Market coveted a country not yet in its clutches, some transparent pretext was found—the suppression of a slavery different from, and not so cruel as that of commerce; the pushing of a religion no longer believed in by its promoters; the rescue of some desperado or homicidal madman whose misdeeds had got him into trouble amongst the natives of the "barbarous country"—any stick, in short, which would beat the dog at all. Then some bold, unprincipled, ignorant adventurer was found (no difficult task in the days of competition), and he was bribed to "create a market" by breaking up whatever traditional society there might be in the doomed country, and by destroying whatever leisure or pleasure he found there. He forced wares on the natives which they did not want, and took their natural products "in exchange," as this form of robbery was called, and thereby he "created new wants," to supply which (that is, to be allowed to live by their new masters) the hapless, helpless people had to sell themselves into the slavery of hopeless toil so they might have something with which to purchase the nullities of "civilization." "Ah," said the old man, pointing to the Museum, "I have read books and papers in there, telling strange stories indeed of the dealings of civilization (or organized misery) with non-civilization; from the time when the British Government deliberately sent blankets infected with small-pox as choice gifts to inconvenient tribes of Red-skins, to the time when Africa was infested by a man named Stanley, who . . ."

This theme may seem out-moded now. For myself, I never grow tired of contemplating the comedy, and I favour here a quotation from H.E.

In the nineteenth century there lived at the extremity of South America a race of people, wholly untouched by the outside world, who had yet attained to a high degree of culture of their own. They possessed a complex and elaborate language;

their oral literature, poetry, and folklore was of the highest interest; they had carried an ideal of courtesy, democracy, and reverence for mental superiority to a point still unknown to the Europe of their time; they were naked in spite of the cold, and lived on whale blubber, and their simple implements were more efficient under the conditions of their life than the most complicated machine-made articles. European visitors were of course impressed by the degradation in which these people lived; they were "savages of the lowest grade." So the usual English missionary was sent out. With great energy he rapidly converted them, clothed them, built houses for them, with the result that in a few years they all died of consumption and pneumonia. A people that from time immemorial had had a free and independent life was, under the influence of European civilization, reduced by the end of the nineteenth century to a handful of broken-spirited individuals in a mission house, and the missionary was left the pious task of gathering together the records of their culture. The same experiment had been carried out, with the same results, in almost every quarter of the globe, and one can but admire the dogged persistency of these Europeans, their blind faith in themselves, their sublime indifference to facts.

The Nineteenth Century: A Dialogue in Utopia is a short book, too soon over, but it covers a great deal of H.E.'s ideas concerning the position of science and philosophy; of archaeology and anthropology; of architecture and aesthetics; of patriotism, lawyers, and journalists; of sex and of moral force; and of the art he favoured most—the art of living. It is written mostly in a vein of irony, so that all of it gives pleasure. "They never killed their young unmarried mothers until they had first forced them to destroy their babies"; "I do not see how sex could ever have been impure to people who have lived among flowers—and that has been always"; " 'Moral force' was thus you see, a very curious thing, at once social and anti-social; it was not exactly insanity, nor criminality; it was just 'moral force.' " The charm of such saying will always endure.

Near the end he has a passage to which personally, I often return to regain my balance when I have lost my perpendicular in a gust of wind—which is not infrequently in the mental atmosphere of our day. Its great merit is that it is meaningless to those who are angry with the world in the wrong way. "I begin to see the characteristics of that age. But I scarcely know even yet whether one ought to bless or to curse it," says one of the two Speakers. "One can never do either," the other replies.

"It is a bad world, may be, but there could not be a better world. Life has always been perfect. The sum of satisfaction can scarcely be greater in any age than it has been in any other age. To cut off the channels of human satisfaction is but to concentrate and intensify the satisfaction which gushes through the few channels that are left. The morality of men, or their immorality, may have perverted their vision, or driven them to every excess of cruelty, but who can say that they were therefore less happy? If there are born martyrers, there are born martyrs as well. The exuberance of life has never failed. We shudder with horror as we gaze back at the brutality of the past. But they never shuddered. They were engaged in a perpetual battle, but when a man was struck it is only we, the spectators, who are hurt; they fought on, unknowing their wounds. Our emotions as we gaze at the Lancashire Enclosure have nothing in common with the emotions of the inhabitants. Even the restless discontent that can never die is a part of perfection; for without it there could not be that perpetual slight novelty which alone makes life different from death. And those who have most suffered have ever been those who were least discontented. The wisdom that comes of suffering has taught them how little change means. Life has always been perfect.

"Is it not another way of saying that life can never be perfect?"

"Yes, that was my thought. There is but a hair's-breadth between us and the nineteenth century. If we had quite reached perfection there would be nothing left but death; if they had not almost touched it, they could not have lived at all. Food was always sweet to them, how sweet we may estimate by the immense energy they expended to obtain a morsel of it; man has always been a tormenting joy to woman, and woman to man;

it was good to have children; the spectacle of Nature was always there to bring consolation and rest to those who could see it; at the worst man could lose himself in some vast dream. And all these things were possible, even when men were living on the edge of starvation and crushed beneath the tyranny of machinery. All that we count civilization has but filled in graciously the intervals of life. It may have helped to harmonize human passions; it has not made sweeter the gratification of those passions. Make earth like hell as much as you can, and all the deepest passions of man can still find satisfaction. He could desire no more in heaven. One may even doubt sometimes whether we have added anything to life which adequately compensates for the obstacles which the modern world sets in the way of those passions for which the 'progressive' conditions of the nineteenth century offered so magnificent a field, such elemental passions as hate and greed and pride and lust."

And when the little Dialogue closes we are left, not dispirited by an empty dream of happiness or a vile vision of misery and degradation; but with the truth about humanity in all ages and in all countries, whether in England or Germany, in Japan or Russia: "And as they passed up the slope still discoursing on life and death, they heard the soft laughter of young men and maidens among the trees, as it always has been, as it always will be, through the brief day of Man's life on earth."

16

THIS brings us up to 1900, when he was forty-one. He was to live for nearly another forty years. His work went steadily ahead, while the external events (for the next sixteen years) were chiefly confined to grappling with his wife. Those familiar with his Autobiography will know that at intervals he refers to "her dear friend of this period." It is understood that he means more than just friendship. These attractions, being basically sexual, never lasted very long on that level, though the friendship was seldom dropped, for she had a gift for friendship as well as for love, which triumphed over disappointment. This is well illustrated when on one occasion she fell in love with a young woman (qualified as a doctor) who at first appeared to return the fascination, but later, realizing the situation and feeling it to be abnormal and alien to her, became cold to all advances. This threw Edith into a state of melancholic depression for months while she brooded over the love she had lost and still sought the means by which she might regain it. She turned, as always, to H.E. for help and consolation, and in the end his sympathy, I think, pulled her out of the depression, and an ordinary affectionate friendship ripened between the two women.

The most remarkable example of sexual inversion on the part of Edith occurred earlier, and I must mention it briefly here on account of the light which it throws on the character of H.E. When they went abroad after the Trial the long in-

terruption caused her passion for Claire to revert to that of
normal friendship. On their return to England there was no
woman upon whom she could lavish a passionate attention.
It was at this time that Lily came into her life. Lily was an
artist of modest pretensions who lived at St. Ives on a private
income. She was of Scottish-Irish family from Ulster. Edith
for the rest of her life adored everything Irish, taking Lily
as a typical flower of that country. According to H.E. she was
a "creature of fascinating charm that was felt alike by men
and women, by rich and poor." Several of her characteristics
certainly were especially Irish. She was lacking in coarseness:
in her there was a complete absence of vulgarity. There was
a purity about her which rose, not from moral principle,
but by nature. Also, equally Irish, she possessed a vein of
mockery and cruelty, of irresponsibility and unreliability.
She had no strength of character, no will-power, no soul, and
probably not much brain. A woman can be very fascinating to
men, or to women, without these properties. H.E. says that
Edith knew they could never be mates in soul, and though
Lily had no soul (like Thomas Hardy's heroines), Edith
knew that there is a sphere of love in which that counts for
nothing. Lily had an ethereal fragility of body in contrast
to Edith who, though subject to a series of neurotic illnesses,
was sturdy in frame. Lily's fragility and Irish delicacy and
refinement greatly appealed to Edith, for "she felt an intense
repugnance to all grossness in love; even a trace of its presence, or a suggestion of viciousness," H.E. declares, "more
than once brought to naught her nascent attraction to a
woman" (though it is not clear exactly what he means by
this). It is questionable how far Lily loved her, though it is
certain that for a short time at any rate Edith's boyishness
made a great appeal; but it is known that she made fun of
her to others and spoke slightingly of H.E. behind his back.
Her own appeal to Edith was overwhelming, no one ever
satisfied her so completely, no one ever called out her loving
attentions so inventively. When with Lily she became a boy,
not only in air and spirit and eagerness but in poses and

gestures. A subtle change was effected in her attitude to H.E. whom she no longer addressed as "sweetheart." He felt no jealousy. Lily represented something for her with which he could not compete—he might as well have been jealous of a star. And Lily could hardly compete with him—the only person she could rely upon or from whom she could hope for understanding. On one occasion he gave up his studio to them for the day at Hawkes Point. Lily was closely guarded by her elder sister who took a dim view of Edith, and it was always with difficulty that they met alone. Sometimes she would arrive at Carbis late, after she had been given up; and perhaps they had only one perfectly happy night together, a certain night in October which was ever afterwards remembered by Edith in a halo of beauty, held each year as the anniversary of the most sacred hours of her life.

Time never spoilt this idyll for her. Lily was dead in a year or two—victim of Bright's disease at the age of thirty-six. Thus it was possible for Edith to cherish a perfect memory. It gradually became far more than this. It became the worship of an image forever radiant and unstained. Lily's portrait was always beside her, and anything she had been given by her was cherished with anxious care—a brooch, a cup, a looking-glass, a cushion, a table-cloth. She did not worship her only as a memory, but regarded her as a still living person in the next world, in touch with her to guide and to console. For the remaining fourteen years of her life she communicated with Lily through a medium, though she had no particular taste for spiritualism save in this one particular. Lily spoke to her in what seemed her natural voice, gave advice, foretold the future, and uttered words of love and encouragement to fortify her resolutions. Edith was not led astray by this; she kept her head, prepared to believe that there was deception, but since she wished to believe in the authenticity of these communications she found it easy to do so. Sometimes, without a medium, she would have visitations from Lily's spirit, becoming conscious of her presence in the room at Carbis. H.E. took no part in this. But he was not discouraging or contemptuous. He did not try to explain away her experiences. He said that his mind was always open. Seeing that her head was not turned and that she remained sensible, he was glad that she should have this worship.

Years after reading H.E.'s Autobiography for the first time (in 1940), a number of passages, it is needless to say, remained in my mind: I think of one especially now, so characteristic of him, so unlike the thought, or phrasing, of anyone else. That seems to me a good reason for including it here. It comes at the close of his account of Edith and Lily:

I am always tolerant to what is natural and sincere. But in this matter my attitude was more than that of toleration, it was nearer to reverence. I realized that in his revelation of Lily as a source of spiritual succour Edith was making her nearest approach to the consoling power of mysticism. She was not naturally possessed of the mystical temper, much less so than I am. To me it had come in youth through a natural interior development, with no strong impulse from without. She was rebellious to such development. Her egoism was too strong, her sensibilities too acute, her temper too dominant and energetic for the mystical spirit to be natural or easy to her. It could only come through the crushing shock of love swiftly passing to loss, and even then she was never entirely subdued to it. But such as it was, it was her religion, the only real religion she ever had, the true heaven of her soul, and there was nothing for me to feel but reverence.

No doubt the fact that Lily was a woman and not a man made this easier for H.E. He was never called upon to be made jealous of other men. Shortly after the death of Lily, an admirer of Amy's, considering himself aggrieved, sought to revenge himself upon H.E. He sent a manuscript to Edith under a transparent disguise, purporting to reflect H.E.'s relations with Amy. The facts were not in question, and were known to Edith, but in this "account" plausible suggestions and perversions of truth were woven into the bare facts with a maximum of vulgarity in a manner most calculated to make him look ridiculous. When Edith read this malicious document she fell to the ground.

It appears also that the writer of the letter had actually employed a private detective to watch the movements of H.E. At that time all the detective could observe was his client going regularly to the British Museum Reading Room. This was very unsatisfactory material, and since he possessed no ticket for admission he could not get into the room himself to conduct further research, and was obliged to wait in the vestibule or stand on the steps and contemplate the disdainful countenance of Hoa-Haka-Nana-Ia from Easter Island. But one day it seemed that he was to get a break. Edith had come up to London with her maid, Priscilla, and had to leave early next morning for Manchester to give a lecture. Would Havelock show Priscilla round London? She arranged that he would. It was an extensive day of sight-seeing—Westminster Abbey, the National Gallery, the Museum, St. Paul's, the Temple, Charing Cross foot-bridge and so on. The exhausted detective could do little with this, but he rose to the occasion and reported that H.E. was leading "a very immoral life with women."

It was characteristic of Edith that she decided to be "deeply wounded" by that letter, and she let it rankle, and from time to time she found it useful as a weapon of offence, but it did no real harm to anyone concerned except the sender who therewith assured his complete exclusion from Amy's life. For the next ten years H.E. and Edith grew closer, which was partly due to the fact that she was often ill and he was her devoted nurse. His account of this is not thrilling but it is touching, and it will always touch those whom it concerns— that is to say, those who have done likewise, and those who are ready to see that it can be done.

17

WHILE the *Studies* were being written and published, he was also writing and publishing other books, *The Nineteenth Century*, for example, which was followed in 1904 by a *Study of British Genius* which came just after Volume III of the *Studies*. It is an elaborate analysis of the eminent men and women of Britain from the sixteenth to the end of the nineteenth century. There are representatives from actors, divines, doctors, lawyers, men of letters, men of science, musical composers, philosophers, poets, politicians, sailors, scholars, soldiers and travellers. He chose a cross-section out of one thousand and seventy-six men and forty-six women, and examined their regional character, social class, heredity and parentage, childhood and youth, marriage and family, duration of life, pathology, stature, pigmentation and other characteristics. The book is full of interesting facts: thus, to take a single example, there is a table exhibiting the percentage of illnesses as distributed over the various groups showing that Divines are subject to more ill health than any other group. It seems that Galton, having analysed the 196 biographies contained in Middleton's *Biographia Evangelica*, came to the conclusion that there is "a frequent correlation between an unusually devout disposition and a weak constitution." On the subject of genius and insanity he reaches the conclusion that the real affinity of genius is with congenital imbecility rather than with insanity—which strikes me as being far from surprising.[1]

This book, with all its interest, yet seems to me hardly worth the labour. I grudge the time he spent on it—on the formidable appendices alone! He himself complains of the toil he had to endure on account of the defects of the *Dictionary of National Biography*. He had expected to obtain from those volumes the data which he needed. "I soon realized, however, that the biographers were, with a few notable exceptions, literary men, unfamiliar with biological methods, and that they had seldom realized that biography is not a purely literary recreation, and that it demands something more than purely literary aptitudes." Thus in order to supplement the information furnished by the *Dictionary* he was obliged to consult over three hundred biographies as well as many other sources of information in memoirs and personal reminiscences. No wonder he wrote that celebrated "Open Letter to Biographers"[2] in a tone of bitterness and hostility seldom displayed in his writing. Biography was a form of literature he was most ready to find of fascinating interest and of profound instruction. "Paint them as they are, paint them as they are!" he exclaimed again in nearly the last entry in the third volume of *Impressions and Comments*. One of the sources of his hostility towards them was their attitude of apology for, or mockery of, weakness of character. He held that for the highest genius weakness was essential; it allowed a place of entrance for the breath of inspiration—an opening not provided by men of "strong character." This, it will be remembered was also put forward emphatically by Keats in his *Letters*. H.E. returns to this many times in the course of his books, his last mention of it being, I think, when he came to Rousseau in his survey of French literature, called *From Rousseau to Proust*. It is one of those splendid truths which are perfectly obvious—

---

[1] See in this connection Shaw's *The Sanity of Art* in reply to Max Nordan's *Degeneration*.
[2] See *Views and Reviews*, Vol. I.

after they have been stated. I must make room here to quote
H.E.'s neatest statement of it (in *Impressions and Comments*,
Vol. I). He first speaks of the Russian philosopher, Schestoff,
who pointed out that while we have to be reticent regarding
the weaknesses of ordinary men, we can approach the great
with open eyes and need never fear to give their qualities
the right names. "How simply and quietly," he says, "the
Gospel reports that in one night the Apostle Peter denied
his Master thrice! And yet that has not hindered mankind
from building him a magnificent temple in Rome, where un-
told millions have reverently kissed the feet of his statue, and
even today his representative is counted infallible."

It is a pregnant observation [writes H.E.] that we might well
bear in mind when we concern ourselves with the nature and
significance of genius. I know little about St. Peter's claim to
genius. But at least he is here an admirable symbol. That is how
genius is made, and, it is interesting to note, how the popular
mind realizes that genius is made; for the creators of the Gospels, who have clearly omitted or softened so much, have yet
emphatically set forth the bald record of the abject moral failure
in the moment of decisive trial of the inappropriately named
Rock on which Christ built His Church. And Peter's reputation
and authority remain supreme to this day.

James Hinton was wont to dwell on the weakness of genius,
as of a point of least resistance in human nature, an opening
through which the force of Nature might enter the human
world. "Where there is nothing there is God," and it may be
that this weakness is no accident but an essential fact in the
very structure of genius. Weakness may be as necessary to the
man of genius as it is unnecessary to the normal man.

Our biographers of genius are usually futile enough on all
grounds, even in the record of the simplest biological data, as in
my own work I have had sad occasion to experience. But at no
point are they so futile as in toning down, glozing over, or altogether ignoring all those immoralities, weaknesses, defects, and
failures which perhaps are the very hall-mark of Genius. They
all want their Peters to look like real rocks. And on such rocks
no churches are built.

When saying that I grudged the time which H.E. spent over the—to me—rather unfruitful donkey-work of the *Study of British Genius*, I was thinking of his abilities as a Critic of Literature in the broadest sense—abilities which belonged to him alone, since he could bring so many instruments to bear upon his subject, by no means least the science of ethnology. A particularly good example of this is the chapter—added later to *British Genius*—called "The Celtic Spirit in Literature." This is one of the most searching essays he ever wrote. Having disposed of the Celts, *per se*, by pointing out that no one knows what a Celt is exactly or where the creature is to be found definitely, he goes on to say that we can define the Celtic Spirit as a love of decoration, and, as the chief thing, a love of *the remote as remote*. The opposite to this is what he calls the Nordic spirit which loves the present, and when it deals with the remote wants to make it *present*—which is abhorrent to the Celtic spirit. He defines the latter as being chilled with the real scene and only able to describe that which it *has not seen*, while the Nordic is only at ease with the immediate—"I was there, I saw it." I think that is profoundly helpful. He then maintains that we cannot now possibly say that the Celtic spirit is to be found *here* and the Nordic spirit *there*, for during recent centuries the blood-streams have flowed together and been mixed together so inextricably that this is the clue to our literature, and accounts for Shakespeare. Personally, I endorse this heartily. I never understood Shakespeare until I read H.E.'s essay on this subject. For there is so much in Shakespeare that makes one think that he must have come from Dublin! Then one thinks of his other opposite qualities which can only be accounted for by his coming from Warwickshire. It explains Shaw who was compulsively attracted to the Nordic preference for the immediate and the real while at the same time being terrified by the Celtic strain that could so easily lull him into being the idle singer of an empty day. And, if I may say so in passing, it explains myself to myself in this at least that I can equally revere G.B.S. and H.E.—this being easier for me coming from County Dub-

lin and educated in England, than for some one born in Tooting or Camberwell.

At the close of his essay on the Celtic Element in Literature,
H.E. observes that he has said nothing of "the Celtic Movement," and he suggests that the reason may perhaps be clear.
There is no Celtic Movement. Nor are great poets the outcome of such movements. Of course we immediately think
of Yeats. Yeats, by the way, was fond of saying that he didn't
understand Shaw and that Shaw hadn't a clue to the Yeatsian
mind. In my opinion Yeats understood Shaw perfectly well,
and in his last period went Shaw's early way with good results—while Shaw in his old age merely went downhill (not
that it mattered). "If at the present time we possess one poet
at all events who adequately represents the Celtic spirit," H.E.
winds up his essay in his most magisterial manner—which I always enjoy—preferring not to mention Yeats by name, "it is
equally true that the same poetic qualities may be traced
throughout the whole of our literature. This is clear even to
one who has, personally, no part or lot in the Celtic world.
It may indeed be said that until we realize clearly what the
Celtic spirit means we are without the clue to guide us through
our literature. Sagacious observers in the past have from time
to time vaguely seen the significance, now of this element,
now of that, possibly even of both. But the literary historian
of the past has failed to grasp that significance in any broad or
definite manner. The clue can only be found when we place
ourselves at a standpoint at once psychological and ethnological. As we follow it, our rich and varied literature, for the
first time, falls into harmonious order."

At this point I may with advantage take up a question
which has always bothered me—not that I can hope to answer
it. Speaking of Havelock Ellis, H.L. Mencken said, "the
extent of his knowledge is appalling." To me it is incom-
prehensible. I do not know how he managed to absorb
what he did and at the same time write books. Every occasion
when I take him up the same question confronts me—how did

he do it? I daresay I am easily awed by learned men. By Spengler, for example; though I am awed not only by his knowledge but by his titanically Teutonic absence of art and grace. And there are others of course. But I do not think that their range is in the same category as that of H.E.'s. Indeed, I am free to say frankly that I do not believe that any other man's range has ever been so *assured*. It really was as if he had said, with Bacon—I will take all knowledge for my province. Bacon may or may not have done so, but he had three hundred years less reading to get up. Of course H.E. did *not* take all knowledge for his province. His mind did not move freely in the realm of mathematics. He was weak on ornithology. He may not have known all about beetles. In fact he deliberately determined to absorb nothing that he could not absorb fully, to have as few as possible broken bits and pieces of knowledge stuck about his mind—that in itself is an important achievement for any man. But it is truly appalling, as Mencken justly said, to contemplate the extent of the territory over which he elected to range with calm assurance. When we read through his two volumes of *Views and Reviews*, for instance, we find speciality after speciality, whether it be anthropology or mythology or ethnology or archaeology or French Literature or the Dutch novel or German philosophy or criminology or Russian revolutionaries or psychoanalysis, viewed with the serene coolness, temperance, and sympathy of a man who appears to have got the subject in easy perspective *and* to have read the latest authorities upon it, no matter in what language they were written. In other books such as the *Impressions* or *The Dance of Life* or *The Genius of Europe* we find equally remarkable his historical knowledge; his genealogical and ethnological flair; his grasp of the literature of all the nations; his up-to-this-very-hour-dateness regarding the new physics. We turn over the leaves and we begin to think that the subject upon which he is most searching is architecture. Then we think that perhaps his insight into the painting of the world is the main thing—until we turn to his remarks on music. To the reader who is unfamiliar with much of H.E.'s work, this will sound clumsy exaggeration; to the reader who is familiar with the works it will seem a clumsy attempt to give some idea of the range.

The question remains—how did he do it? For *at the same time* he carried out his chief life work, the seven volumes of the *Studies*—and also wandered extensively over the Continent. He himself gives us little help in answering this question. He says, on several occasions, that he never worked at all: he only played. He was just "a dreamer lying in the sunshine." We know what he means. For him work was play and play was work: all the things which others consider recreation from work, such as games of any kind whatsoever, social gatherings, gossip in pubs, detective novels, all the many pass-the-times known to the average man, he left on one side. We grant also that there was here a special genius, the genius of absorption, which like all genius, gives the impression of *effortlessness*. Even so, I still do not understand it. I am aware that Churchill has not only lived that wonderful life, but has written all those famous volumes—it seems the act of a superman, and is, up to a point. Yet I can understand this. He could employ, or rather, deploy, a platoon of secretaries and research workers to do the donkey-work, to lay hold of the facts he wanted, assemble them, and hand them over. Then he could give them shape—by dictation if necessary. It is not easy to give anything shape, it calls for that anvil and that forge; but to lay hold of the material, to know where to look for it, to haul it out of the libraries, to study it—this is a great labour and time-devourer. And this is chiefly what I do not understand about H.E.—even the technical business of his having the right books with him as he sat on a cliff in Cornwall or in the Australian Bush. I could understand it better if he had been one of those people who like Macaulay, could read a page at the pace most people take to glance down it, and remember it all. Yet I cannot associate that sort of faculty with H.E. It seems foreign to that elephantine slow motion, to that lack of haste which he always displayed— and I think also that an exceptional memory does not go well with the faculty of imagination, or the capacity to think profoundly, or to experience with receptivity, or to contemplate calmly. A friend of mine has suggested that H.E. can only be explained on the theory of reincarnation. He had been here before and could somehow pick it all up in a minute or had it all with him—if so, I wonder who he was? Then I look at the plants. Perhaps they can help. They are toiling all the time. Without haste, but also without rest. Nothing interferes with their absorption: no side-issues, no moments of idleness, no time wasted, no blind alleys, no parties, no motor drives: just steady work with an innate capacity for creative synthesis all the time. Perhaps he was like that. But I hold it against H.E. that while he makes it clear in his Autobiography that he let nothing prevent him from carrying out his work, he fails to tell us anything about his methods of work.

18

I HAVE spoken of his wanderings abroad. The country that he visited most often was Spain which had an unfailing attraction for him. His book, *The Soul of Spain*, was first published in 1908 and reprinted twelve times. He felt that he knew and loved Spain better than any other European country—not even excepting France. Spain has always appealed to the English. It may be said that the English are so English that they are eager to throw off their Englishness whenever the opportunity offers. This tendency cannot be said so emphatically about the members of any other nation. They do it even in England on occasion (and if there is a heat wave they go slightly off their heads). But they can unloosen their tightness more unobtrusively abroad and happily join with those who move to a different tempo and a less principled outlook—especially in Spain. H.E. was an intensely English person in so many ways, and Spain was just what he needed for refreshment of spirit.

It has been supposed that the English could, and as a matter of fact they do, refresh themselves with the ethos of the Irish in much the same way—which is not surprising seeing that the Iberian element is still flourishing in Ireland. H.E. tells a story as recorded by a Spanish magistrate and reported in an Aragonese newspaper at a time of economic distress in Aragon. A labourer was determined to rob the first person he met on the highroad. He came upon a man with a wagon and instantly demanded his money. "Here are thirty dollars, all that I have," said the man. "There is nothing for me but robbery, my family are dying of hunger," declared the robber apologetically, pocketing the cash. Then his mind changed, "Take this, *chico*," he said, giving back twenty-nine dollars, "one is enough for me." "Would you like anything I have in the cart?" asked the waggoner. "Yes. Take this dollar back too, I had better have some rice and some beans." The waggoner gladly handed over a bag of vegetables, and then offered the man five dollars—which was declined. "Take them for luck-money," pressed the waggoner, "I owe you that." And only so was the would-be robber persuaded to accept.

That story would be totally out of place concerning any-one anywhere in England. It is, strictly, inconceivable among the English, contrary to their whole bend and general angle of approach to life. In the first place, the aggressor in England would never have given back the money, and in the second place if he had, the waggoner would not have given him any-thing out of the cart nor offered him a few shillings. He would have felt it "well within his rights to inform the police" when he got to town. But the story would be quite in order if recorded as an Irish scene to this day. In fact I have some-times told it, adopting the Irish brogue and adding and altering a few words idiomatically in the dialogue, to English friends as an Irish story. It has seemed "very Irish" to them —as indeed it is. We often hear about "the funny Irishman" and "the fiery Irishman spoiling for a fight." I have puzzled over this, thinking that a kind of melancholy gentleness is more evident in their personal contacts. Writing of the Spanish, H.E. says—"We are not unaccustomed to find a veneer of humanity and courtesy over an underlying violence and hardness, but in this temperament it is the violence and hard-ness which lie nearer to the surface, and they fall away at once as soon as human relationships are established." Those words, whether read by a Spaniard or an Irishman, come as a revelation.

Though H.E. travelled a great deal he never wrote a travel

book—not even a few articles to pay his expenses. The fact
is he felt himself incompetent to write anything that was not a
personal *need* to write. He felt that he could and should write
upon the Women of Spain. His comments were fortified
by personal impressions but not particularized by personal
contacts (perhaps he made none?). He loved these journeys
but he gives us no details of them, and it is hard to visualize him in train or street or hotel lounge. He passes
straight to the generalization. He felt he could do this without superficiality. Count Keyserling also could do this, and
though a thundering egotist, he recognized a master in Havelock Ellis. And I have little doubt that H.E. would have hailed
a peer in this line Salvador de Madariaga, the Spaniard who
has chosen to live amongst us and to expose with the hard
light of his genius the danger of our present confusing
postures in relation to the Soviet Union.

In 1905 H.E. paid his most memorable visit to Spain. This
was the occasion on which he stayed for two days in the
Monastery at Montserrat. He did detail his personal experience about this at some length—a great spiritual experience.
He devotes a chapter to it in his *Soul of Spain*, while in his
Autobiography he says how it marked the most prolonged
period of sustained and almost ecstatic exaltation he had ever
reached. He says that for a moment, for an hour, possibly
even for a day, he had sometimes attained such inner joy
before, and maybe since; "but never unless possibly at Sparkes
Creek, has the experience of joyous exaltation been so prolonged, for with that economy of joy, that fear of reaching
the dregs of the cup of pleasure which I must regard as one
of my traits, I left while I might still have spent a day there."
In 1905 this still unspoilt monastery, built on a mountain
side which was not only a shrine of man's but a shrine of
Nature's, was perhaps one of the most exalting spots in the
world. H.E.'s long description of it and experience of his
sojourn there when he rose at five in the morning and walked
along the mountain paths that encircle the Monastery, carries
us into the paradise-lost regions of the mind.

The paths that wind round the mountain towards the summit reveal here and there a neglected chapel, a cave that was once inhabited, a ruined hermitage. Every such spot once had its hermit, and when he died there were always eager candidates for the vacant post. Very sacred is the little cave associated with the name of Garin—a ninth-century saint whose sins were grievous and his life here, it is said, of awful austerity. "It is a common and indeed a commendable custom among Spaniards," wrote James Howell from Madrid, in 1622, in his *Familiar Letters,* "when he hath passed his Grand Climacterie to make a voluntary Resignation of Offices, be they never so great and profitable, and sequestering and weaning themselves, as it were, from all mundane Negotiations and Incumbrances, to retire to some Place of Devotion, and spend the Residue of their Days in Meditation." Very certainly, however, the lives of the world-weary men who came to spend their last years here were not usually without their joys. Even this cave of Garin's, small as it is, stands in an admirably chosen spot and commands a magnificent view. It is impossible not to believe that the men who retired from the conflicts and anxieties of the world to this serene height were not entirely moved, as it seemed to the ignorant mob, by an unquenchable thirst for suffering, or a resolute determination to expiate their sins at all costs. That would have been far better accomplished in less exquisite spots. For many a weary and sensitive soul, we may be sure, it was not the thirst for suffering but the thirst for joy that led them to Our Lady of Montserrat. When they let the heavy burden of the world slide from off their shoulders—the cares of a household, the hardships of camps, the restraints of courts—and climbed to a new home in this mountain, it was not with a sinking, but with a rising heart, with the exhilaration of St. Francis, with the glad new sense of delicious freedom which once filled the men who went into the Thebaid. To lie in the sunshine, and teach the birds to feed from the hand, to know how delicate is the taste of the water one has one's self fetched from the spring, and the herbs one has gathered with care; to watch the superb and ever-changing procession of day and night, of summer and winter; to gaze on the towns and villages that lie along the banks of the Llobregat below and look so insignificant—here was an unfailing source of spiritual joy to men who knew how bitterly tasted the dregs of the cup of life.

19

IT WAS in 1909 that H.E., on being forced to leave his rooms in the Temple on account of the marriage of Arthur Symons, finally took a flat in Brixton—which proved to be his London home for twenty years. Edith and he still had a foothold in Cornwall, now at Moor Cottages. Edith wrote to him about his new flat saying that she thought it sounded good. "Offer them £46 at first and let me one room for £10. Be in it before I come up and I will bring a bed and a few things with me. I should not disturb you a bit as I can always cook my own breakfast etc. . . . If you think £15 fairer I could perhaps manage that, or £12, whichever you think. . . . Don't say you would not like me to have a room in your flat— I wouldn't disturb you." He settled for £10—and always cooked her breakfast. But she didn't keep the room long, for having written a play which was accepted for production, she now had many additional friends and activities in London; and finding it too tiring to get back to Brixton late at night, she took a flat at the top of a doctor's house in Harley Street. This suited him also, he says, since his regular habits and early hours were disturbed by the Brixton arrangement. At Harley Street she was as comfortably as centrally situated, he tells us: "Here I could go to see her, and she could come from time to time to spend a few days at my flat, no longer as a tenant, but as a welcome guest."

We are not meant to smile, I think, at the phrasing of that

last sentence. We are certainly meant, however, to note again that their marriage was not entirely conventional. And elsewhere he insists how they retained their love by not tying it down to place and property, and he observes emphatically how in practice they had lived up to their cherished ideals of freedom and independence in contradistinction to those couples who in the name of duty and convention are afraid to leave each other's side. While we applaud this we are also entitled to remember that if they did not enter into the prison of the home; if they did not contract home-sickness; if they did not load themselves with chains believing them to be garlands, in the usual way—they had no children.

Meanwhile Edith became on friendly terms with all concerned in the production of her play, and this led to an invitation to visit the home of Beryl Faber (the actress who had contributed most to the success of the play) at the village of West Drayton. Close by her house there was another to let, called Woodpecker Farm. It was about three centuries old, out of repair, infested with vermin, and lately discovered as a suitable abode by convicts and vagabonds. Edith was delighted with it. In her mind's eye she instantly saw how it could be transformed into a lovely place where she and H.E. could eventually spend a peaceful old age together, while they would also have Beryl as a charming neighbour. She immediately interviewed the landlady and practically committed herself and him to take over the place at the longest lease possible. Then she told him. He was appalled. There would be too much expense in making the place habitable. She brushed aside his caution. The obstacles only served to fortify her resolution. It was too late to go back honourably, she declared, as she had already committed them to the transaction. If he did not wish to share the responsibility, let him say so, she would not blame him, she would quite understand, don't let him worry, she would find some one else. He yielded. He subdued his feelings at not being previously consulted, and "spent sleepless hours at night over the burden we were assuming that neither of us was really able to bear"

—strong words for H.E. They signed the lease. Before they had even got into the place, as is the way of things, one of the chief attractions for her, the presence of Beryl Faber as a delightful neighbour, was taken away, for Beryl, on account of a disagreement with her landlord, left West Drayton. This sort of thing is normal, and Edith had encountered it before, but she could not learn from experience (nor can I). They went there for two years—defying now, it seems, their ideal of not setting up house together. The cost of its upkeep mounted. It became impossible. But luckily a wealthy American, who had entered the inner circle of Edith's friends, became attracted to the place, and bought it on a liberal scale. H.E. saw nothing of his share in the purchase money. Edith argued that her debts were urgent, while H.E. could wait. Thus his repayment was postponed to an unspecified time—which never came.

H.E. says, at one place in his Autobiography, that he did not know whether he was a weak or a strong character. Like most of us he was both. Here he was weak. He never seems to have been able to take a strong line with her. When she made commitments without consulting him he gave in. He was silent. He staged no scene. He never told her to pipe down. There is a single exception to this—before their marriage. She had written him a silly letter, taking too much liberty. He replied in strong terms. And instantly she did pipe down and behaved herself. His comment upon this letter of his, in the Autobiography, is interesting, and sad. He said that he scarcely recognized himself in it. "At a later period I should have written more tenderly and could not have set the matter forth with such self-possessed precision." I recall a remark made to me by a woman of great ability and charm concerning H.E.'s Autobiography: "So *much* understanding, so *much* compassion! . . ." I think she meant that she would rather be hit over the head. But perhaps it is not very easy for men to satisfy women.

It might fairly be said that H.E. did not understand women very well in this sort of way. Yet—who knows?—he may have felt that he must always be true to his deepest impulse, that he must be emerald, and obey his own nature to be on all such occasions tolerant, patient, forbearing. We may call it weakness. He was also strong. In the *Dance of Life* he dropped the remark, "No man, indeed, can write anything that matters who is not a hero at heart, even though to people who pass him in the street or know him in the house he may seem as gentle as any dove." He may appear mild, but that mildness is deceptive. His determination to get his work done, and to do it in solitude, makes him callous. H.E. was often accused of callousness. He did not deny it. He did not give way. He held to his course.

The two of them certainly made a remarkable contrast. The marriage of contrast is far from an ideal: it can so easily spell hopeless incompatibility. Yet not so here. She needed him as surely as a ship needs ballast. And he said—"What this woman gave me was *life*." But, as I have suggested, people like her do not wear well on paper in future years. They almost invariably give an impression of being phoney. A chairman once referred to her at a public meeting as "the light and hope of civilization." She took it seriously. Her personality worked for her when alive. She was a woman who had "a way with her" as the phrase goes. Her expansiveness was genuine. We get one clear idea of what she was like from Edward Carpenter who was the last man to have tolerated affectation or insincerity or spurious camaraderie. He himself loved talking with farm labourers in his local pub, and was not happy until he had become "accepted" by them—for they are great snobs and seldom unbend towards outsiders as their equals in society. I myself was once accepted by them because I worked with them and was sworn at by the same boss. They do not easily accept a lady on equal terms. Edith paid Carpenter a visit at his place in Millthorpe, and he took her to his pub. He speaks of the impression she made. "The delight and amazement of the farm men of finding someone more or less resembling a lady who really understood and would talk freely about such things (pigs, poultry, and crops)

and her at-homeness among that company, was most re-
freshing. They were fascinated by the directness of her intense blue eyes, her sturdy figure, her vigorous gestures,
and the evident equality of her comradeship with them.
Later they would ask, 'When is that little lady coming again,
with that curly hair, like a lad's, and them blue eyes, what
talked about pigs and cows.' " She might have had a harsh
voice, but it seems to have been of an exceptionally attractive
quality, combined with a ringing laugh. (H.E.'s voice was
disappointing, and I believe he was heard to laugh as seldom
as Walt Whitman. She was just as successful at winning
the hearts of others in quite different classes of society,
while foreigners found it difficult to believe that she was
English, since she lacked the qualities they expected of cold-
ness and formality. (I think the Englishwoman has changed a
good deal in this respect since the nineteenth century.) She
displayed an impulsive helpfulness to others on all sorts of
occasions—while his desire was to be rid of others, and help
them by writing his books. Thus it was probably no exaggeration when he said that he had never known anyone with
so many friends. At the same time she had a bitter and sarcastic
tongue ready to pour out a stream of unjust accusations with
conviction—while H.E. was master of the eloquent silence
and the *not* saying it. It is significant that two of her devoted
maids left the house after a row, never to return or communi-
cate with her again. She put a great strain upon those who
lived continuously with her and H.E. makes it clear that it
was sometimes torture to deal with her. In spite of her sturdi-
ness she was frequently ill (which put her in a powerful
position), though she always recuperated with remarkable
celerity.

She was extreme in her expressions of endearment, while
H.E. declares that never in the course of his life did he address
anyone as "dearest"—for that would seem excessive. If she
had two glasses of wine she would wish for a third: H.E.
believed that two glasses were more than three, and stuck to
two. She was seldom calm. It is thought that calmness was

H.E.'s speciality: calmness and serenity. There is serenity in his work, and we can gain some serenity from reading him. But it is a hardly won quality. It often means that the man is master of his passion, holding it down. There is your artist with a "temperament" upon which he actually trades, and is thought to have more feelings than the quiet man in the corner to whom no one pays any attention because he keeps his feelings in check, whether in office or home—and gets no credit for it. True temperament starts where temperamentals leave off, just as heroism starts where heroics leave off, and piety starts where piousness leaves off, and virtue starts where virtuousness leaves off (a truth understood by few women). H.E. was a passionate spirit. He held his passion down. He gave it no rein on the surface; and the result is that it vibrates through all his work however "reasonable" and "judicious" and cool it may appear—perhaps especially when he was being particularly cool.

She loved company and belonged to clubs. He could not bring himself to enter one. She was a member of the Lyceum Club, but rather than go inside when he wanted to meet her in town, he would arrange to join her at some Underground Station nearby. When it was proposed that a dinner should be held to celebrate his seventieth birthday, presided over by H.W. Nevinson, he felt impelled to decline the honour. The contrast between him and his wife is most complete in their reactions to appearance on the platform. She adored the limelight. This was something he could not bear. He was shy to the point of real weakness. In his *Study of British Genius* there is a notable passage concerning the shyness, bashfulness, and timidity of so many eminent persons. "Some had to abandon the profession they had chosen on account of their nervous shyness at appearing in public; others were too bashful to declare their love to the women they were attracted to; Sir Thomas Browne, one of the greatest masters of English prose, was so modest that he was always blushing causelessly; Hooker, one of the chief luminaries of the English Church, could never look anyone in the face; Dryden, the recognized prince of the literary men of his time, was, said Congreve, the most easily put out of countenance of any man he had ever met." H.E. goes on to suggest why timidity—yet allowing for the fact that none are so bold as the timid when fairly roused—should be especially associated with intellectual aptitudes. "It causes a distaste for social contact and so favours those forms of activity which may be exerted in solitude." There is a good deal of self-revelation here. He seldom could look anyone squarely in the eye: he was afraid of what secrets he might surprise. He found anything in the nature of a social gathering distasteful, being in possession of no small talk—nor did he shine in a salon where there was big talk. He seems to have had no craving for conversation and the clarification of views under the stimulus of opposition or agreement. He would not have welcomed an Eckermann. He could not have tolerated a Boswell. He shocked poor Arthur Symons by saying that he did not want to meet so-and-so, some tremendously well-known literary personage of the moment— "wouldn't cross the street to speak to him." Early in their marriage he was so distressed at the number of people Edith invited as visitors (which included Shaw) that she had to give it up.

But he did occasionally attempt to meet some people. When he was in the Temple he nearly met George Moore. "I will be pleased if you will come and dine with me on Thursday evening," writes Moore in 1898. On Thursday morning came another note written on Wednesday evening. It ran, "I waited dinner half an hour but you did not come. I suppose you forgot. I thought we could have gone to the meeting after dinner." H.E. wrote at once to explain that the misunderstanding was not on his part. Moore did not reply. The invitation was not renewed. H.E. did not write again. And to this hour no man knows what that "meeting" was about. He nearly met Cunninghame Graham, one of the original and fantastic personalities of the age—and I remember so clearly once seeing him in the British Museum Reading Room, erect as a lamp-post as he dealt with the catalogues (which W.B.

Yeats declared were too heavy to hold). He was a considerable writer and a great horseman: he could certainly have claimed to be more of a writer than H.E. was of a horseman, though the latter did once ride on a horse for twenty miles in Australia without falling off, his guide going especially slow in order to accommodate him. During one of his journeys in Spain, H.E. came to a hotel where Cunninghame Graham used to stay, but he was not there then. "I was sorry," says H.E., "for he was a man I should like to meet; I have since heard from a common friend that he would like to meet me; but the meeting has never come about." He also wanted to meet Tolstoy. When in Russia he had an invitation from Tolstoy to visit Yasnaya Polyana. He was about to take the train when he received a mesage from Tolstoy to say that his daughter was ill with typhoid fever—and the chance was lost forever. This was a real disappointment, for H.E. wanted to get a personal impression of him. He regarded him as a superb artist who yet was never himself an artist in life. He considered that Tolstoy fell into "all sorts of mistakes that were almost childish. From first to last he showed no such judgment in the real world as in the world of fiction. He never, to the end, brought love and harmony even into his own household. He never even to the end brought harmony into his own soul. In his work we are amazed at the intellectual force he displayed: in real life his intellectual judgements were prejudiced and unbalanced and narrow."[1] To this judgment H.E. adds a characteristic summing up—in the sense that it is uncharacteristic of anyone else. The simplicity and the cadence could surely be recognized only as his. "It is reported that Tolstoy did not much care either for Shakespeare or Goethe, and it is a significant fact. He was a very great artist. But he was not among the whole men. He was not, even, where he so much desired to be, among the holy men." We might say of Havelock Ellis that he was among the whole men, certainly among the harmonious men; and I would claim that he was, where he never thought about being, among the holy men.

[1] *My Confessional.*

20

THE next book which he brought out was *The World of Dreams*. It was one of his many books for which he had collected material over the years. In his boyhood he had once given pain by saying that it was foolish to tell one's dreams. I have myself expressed just the same boredom at dream-telling. But H.E. remembered it with a pang of regret, and, to make good, he systematically took notes of his own dreams and gathered up a collection of other people's dreams, upon the foundation of which he wrote this book. He does not claim that it is a large garden which he has cultivated—"yet every part of it, I sometimes think, might lead at last to the heart of the universe." And indeed, when the reader puts down the book he may well feel that a window has been opened through which he may gaze into the infinite.

And in a narrower sense a layman, such as myself, can with the help of H.E. gain a foothold here against being swept away by Freud in one direction only. No one can read Freud without being won over by his flair, his genius; but it is obvious that he was inflicted with an intense longing for the *absolute* statement, the generalization that admits of no qualification. This is particularly evident in his insistence that behind the symbolism of dreams there lies ultimately a *wish*. A dream is a wish-fulfillment, and of a more or less sexual kind. H.E. disposes of this view with immense coolness and thoroughness, and, indeed, narrows Freud's field down by about half. "Those who imagine that all dreaming is a symbolism which a single cypher will serve to interpret," he observes, "must not be surprised if, however unjustly, they are thought to resemble those persons who claim to find on every page of Shakespeare a cypher revealing the authorship of Bacon"; and he holds over against the wish-dream the quite distinct contrast-dream in which characteristics emerge altogether opposed to the dreamer's own character and habits, a good example of which he was able to supply from his own experience when on four consecutive nights he dreamed that he was the Mayor of a large northern city about to take the chair at a local meeting of the Bible Society; a soldier in the heat of battle; and a young man meditating about taking the step of going on the stage as a comedian.

Sleeping consciousness is a world scarcely less vast than that of waking consciousness. In so far as we all enter into that world, no reader of *The World of Dreams*, crammed with particular examples grouped into ten chapters by the artist, can fail to be enlightened and enriched, perhaps in the end even asking with Sir William Petty whether there is really any difference between waking and sleeping, or declaring with Godfernaux that though dreams may be delusions, all life is a series of systematised delusions, and that we are in fact "such stuff as dreams are made on." At least we can learn to say with Marcus Aurelius, "When thou hast roused thyself from sleep thou hast perceived that they were only dreams which troubled thee. Now in thy waking hours look at these things about thee as thou didst look at thy dreams." To which H.E. adds the comment—"Dreams are true while they last. Can we, at the best, say more of life?"

There are also passages of great interest on the periphery of the subject. One of these is levitation which is experienced by some people not only when asleep but even when fully awake, a subject which has recently been widely discussed since the publication of Richard Church's *Over the Bridge*. Another is the dream-like effect in the procession of visual imagery evoked by certain drugs, notably mescalin (H.E. calls it mescal). It is well known how thoroughly the effects of mescalin have been ventilated by Aldous Huxley in his glowingly alive book, *The Doors of Perception.* In 1898 H.E. carried out an experiment on himself with mescalin just as Huxley did some fifty years later. I will say a word about this here, for while *The World of Dreams* can be got out of the library, H.E.'s long article on mescalin (only referred to in the book) cannot easily be obtained—to wit—"A New Artificial Paradise" published in *The Contemporary Review,* January 1898.[1]

He conducted the experiment when living in the Temple. The effect the drug had upon him was largely internal; he saw inner visions, seldom resembling definite objects, only the semblance. "I would see thick glorious fields of jewels, solitary or clustered, sometimes brilliant or sparkling, sometimes with a dull rich glow. Then they would spring up into flower-like shapes beneath my gaze, and then seem to turn into gorgeous butterfly forms or endless folds of glistening, iridescent, fibrous wings of wonderful insects." Once he was startled to find that it was raining gold. This orgy of vision was mostly internal, but he also saw outward transformations. "The gas-jet, an ordinary flickering burner, seemed to burn with great brilliance, sending out waves of light, which expanded and contracted in an enormously exaggerated manner." The whole room became vivid and beautiful. It was like the difference between a picture and the actual room, a picture by Claude Monet. He asked some others to try the experiment, one of whom was W.B. Yeats who became utterly fascinated by an advertisement of Bovril on the Embankment, and beheld the most delightful dragons puffing out their breath straight in front of them like rigid lines of steam, and balancing white balls at the end of their breath. H.E. summarizes the effects as revealing an optical fairyland where all

[1] See also his article in *The Lancet* on the "Physiological Aspects," Jan. 1898. Also "Mescal: A Study of a Divine Plant," *Popular Science,* May, 1902.

the senses now and again join the play, while the mind itself
remains a self-possessed spectator. This mescalin toxication
differs from other artificial paradises procured by drugs, for
the mescalin drinker remains calm and collected amid the sensory turmoil around him: there is no vague or voluptuous
appeal. It calls for organic soundness and good health for the
complete manifestation of its virtues. It casts a halo of beauty
around the simplest and commonest things. He adds, curiously, "not only the general attitude of Wordsworth but
many of his most memorable words and phrases cannot—one
is tempted to say—be appreciated in their full significance by
one who has never been under the influence of mescal." Thus
this artificial paradise is safe and dignified beyond its peers.
Would habitual consumption be a good or a bad thing?
"That such consumption would be gravely injurious I cannot
doubt," concludes H.E. "Its safeguard seems to lie in the
fact that a certain degree of robust health is required to obtain
any real enjoyment from its visionary gifts. It may at least be
claimed that for a healthy person to be once or twice admitted to the rites of mescal is not only an unforgettable delight but an educational influence of no mean value."

It is notable that it never occurred to H.E. to consider the
matter in the light of a religious experience. Writing fifty
years later, Huxley thought that he had better make this
clear. "I am not so foolish," he said, "as to equate what happens under the influence of mescalin or any other drug, prepared or in the future preparable, with the realization of the
end and ultimate purpose of human life: Enlightenment, the
Beatific Vision." Not the aim of living but the end. "To see
the World as Beauty is the whole End of Living" is H.E.'s
phrase, as we noted earlier. And surely that is so. Only thus
can we dissolve the gritty Problems—as we dissolve salt in
water. Huxley knew this well enough, and it is a sad com-
mentary on our age that anyone reading the discussions and
controversies that followed the publication of his book would
imagine that he had said the opposite to his remark which I

have just quoted. Not a few people actually thought that he was offering a short cut to the Grace of Vision which comes, if it comes at all, as a soothing and lasting peace after a long period of torturing disquietude. They did really think that here was another thing to be had by proxy, and that just as by using a switch we can turn on the electric light so by swallowing a pill we can turn on the Inner Light.

My purpose in writing this book is not to explain Havelock Ellis. Nor have I set myself the impossible task of commenting exhaustively upon all his works. My modest aim is to present him. That is to say I present a tree. We have here a tree with a massive trunk putting forth branches and leaves in every direction. I can show you the tree and label the branches and draw attention to some of the lovely leaves. *The World of Dreams* was published in 1911, *The Task of Social Hygiene* in 1912. Before coming to it I would like to mention another book of his which I have hitherto been unable to fit in, but it comes naturally here as belonging to the same branch of the tree—namely, *The Nationalization of Health*, published in 1892. It can be taken as a preliminary blueprint for the Health Service of our present Welfare State. He gives a survey of the general development of health movements, the treatment of disease, the private practitioner and his attitudes, the hospital system and the hospital of the future, together with specific consideration of typhoid fever in relation to impure water; of blindness and poor sight; of maternity and its perils; of the dentist's place in health-nationalization, and the magnitude of the evil of bad teeth; and of the necessity to introduce a Ministry of Health. His general plea was that the primary conditions of health should be recognized as of first importance to the community (as they had been in past civilizations) and he deplored the tendency to postpone laying the foundations of our social structure while elaborating its pinnacles, and exploring the psychological ramifications of sentiment while remaining ignorant of the course of the main sewers in our city, and polluting the sources of the water we drink. Today these things are the concern of legislation; and if now we are a little less optimistic about the merits of nationalization, and see more actually the limits of a ministry administering health, we recognize the revolution that has taken place now that it is no longer a privilege, for example, to have good teeth—or, more strictly, not have a mouthful of bad ones.

The Task of Social Hygiene is certainly a forbidding title, suggesting an extension of sanitary science, whereas it is a large volume (the British Museum copy has been studied so much that its cover is in bits and has to be tied together with tape) covering a wide field of interest including the status of women and the problem of their emancipation in relation to ideals of romantic love, the significance of the falling birth-rate, eugenics and love, immorality and the law, sex hygiene, the instruction of children, the individual and socialism, and even the importance of an international language. We must follow Nature, for that is where our new ideas come from. Thus the idea of ablution is less in us than in the animals who are scrupulous in hygiene, even the cockroach living on filth washes all day long. He reminds us that the social order needs continual expansion as well as restriction for the sake of its health as much as the body does. It is not at all a question of artificial interference with Nature. For ideals come from Nature—the idea, for instance, of getting the monkeys down from the trees and onto their hindlegs with their front legs as arms. We may "follow in the same path liberating latent forces of life and suppressing those no longer serving present ends of life." He quotes Shakespeare's lines in *The Winter's Tale:*

"Nature is made better by no mean
But Nature makes that mean . . .
. . . This is an art
Which does mend Nature, change it rather, but
The Art itself is Nature."

It does not read easily as poetry, and is best read as a prose apothegm. H.E. quotes the same lines again in "The Conclusion" of *The Dance of Life*, reminding us that the conception is Aristotelian. That this is so, says H.E., is no testimony to Shakespeare's scholarship. "It is merely the proof that we are here in the presence of one of those great ultimate facts of the world which cannot but be sensitively perceived by the finest spirits, however far apart in time and space. Aristotle, altogether in the same spirit as Shakespeare, insisted that the works of man's making, a State, for example, are natural, though art partly completes what Nature is herself sometimes unable to bring to perfection, and even then that man is only exercising methods which, after all, are those of Nature. Nature needs Man's art in order to achieve many natural things, and Man, in fulfilling that need, is only following the guidance of Nature in seeming to make things which are all the time growing by themselves."

Before concluding, I would like to mention his chapter here on "Religion and the Child." I have long held the view that though children are more lively than adults they are less alive, and that while they have a sense of fancy they have as yet no imagination. That famous "child's sense of wonder" has always seemed to me a fallacy, for this belongs to the mystic, and it is absurd and unnatural to credit a child with religious experience. This view of mine may be faulty, but I think there is some sense in it, and I was relieved to find H.E. saying something of the same kind in this chapter. He suggests that religious ideas cannot be accepted or assimilated by children at all, and that they were not made by children or for children, but represent the feelings and experiences and thoughts of grown-up men, and exceptional men at that. He suggests that the child who is pious and concerned about the state of his soul is an unwholesome child, and that if he prefers praying to playing games with his fellows he is less an example of piety than a cause of parental anxiety with regard to his spiritual condition; and he holds that to preach religious duties to children is not better than to exhort them to imagine themselves married people and to inculcate on them the duties of that relation. "Fortunately the normal child is usually able to resist these influences. It is the healthy child's influence either to let them fall with indifference or to apply to them the instrument of his merciless logic."

21

IN 1914 before the First War had broken out, in March to be exact, H.E. paid a visit to Italy and France and was among the last persons to see the original Rheims Cathedral intact. In Florence he had met Olive Schreiner again. "I found her in fair health and spent ten days there. Then I went on alone for a few days at Ravenna and Bologna." That is all he has to say about his meeting with her. It is clear that she had begun to harden. And one of the saddest and harshest of all facts in the relation between men and women is this—that as women grow older their hearts grow harder and as men get older their hearts get softer.

It was also in this year that Edith planned and executed her first journey to the United States. Through her connection with the Lyceum Club and as the wife of Havelock Ellis who was a good deal better known in America than in England at this time she began to get in touch with American editors and lecture agencies. She had piled up debts and it seemed that she might retrieve the situation by an American lecturing tour. She was encouraged in this by Lily, whose spirit she imagined was suggesting it. Through a medium she received vivid messages from the manifestation of Lily urging her to go, and promising success. She decided to do so, and in a month or two in this same year had boarded a boat at Southampton—with £10 in hand to meet expenses in America. During the two days that had passed since bidding her fare-

well at Brixton (he did not go to Southampton, for her "dear
woman friend of that period" was to say goodbye at the
boat) he received six letters from her. He also received three
more letters from her during the voyage. She had written
them in advance and had given them to the Club porter with
instructions to post at regular intervals during the time she
would be at sea. He received them in the order in which they
were written and intended to arrive, and yet he could discern no apparent numbering on the envelopes. Years later,
when she was no longer alive, it occurred to him to remove
the stamps—and there he found beneath each stamp the date
when the letter should be posted, dates to which the post-
marks corresponded. It is an incident I have been unwilling to
omit. For if from time to time we take the liberty to decide
against her, a thing like this wins us back again. H.E. quotes a
few extracts from these letters, and then he adds, the author
of the seven volumes of *Studies in the Psychology of Sex*,
adds—"And the wonder of it was that all this love and
tenderness and passion on a sea of adventures, apart or together, then and throughout, was on both sides without, in
the narrow physical sense, any elements of sexual emotion!
We neither of us thought of that aspect of it at the time.
When one loves one cannot analyse love. But now, as I look
back, I feel all the novelty and the fascination of it as well as
its instructiveness."

She did well in America. For America did well by her, as
by him, as by so many. "The beautiful hospitality, the unfailing cordiality, the simple helpfulness of Americans—for
which her warm gratitude and admiration never ceased—
surrounded her from the first moment." She was fascinated
by the vitality of the place, the love of knowledge, the respect
for accomplishment, the interest, the enthusiasm, the lack of
inertia, the upward movement, which makes such a glorious
atmosphere for all who come from the Old World. They
took care of her, they made a lioness of her, they praised her
voice saying that it held them spellbound, and loved a lecture
she gave on Havelock Ellis. In her letters to him no words

could express her joy in the wonder of that new civilization
—"Oh, Lily, Lily, how well you knew, and how wonderful it
all is." She was surrounded by adulation, receiving strange
compliments such as a chairman announcing her as "a prophet-
ess from the wilderness, neither wholly woman nor wholly
man but wholly human," which she passed back to H.E. with
the same pleasure as she did that other chairman-remark about
her being "the hope and light of modern civilization." The
truth is, he said, "She was revelling in the environment that
most completely suited her, and she was organizing the
future, an occupation in which she always delighted, and
which had not in it the tiring strain of actual execution."

There was one cloud. She was interviewed a good deal by
journalists. She enjoyed this a lot and became excessively expansive, even in answering personal questions with regard to
her relations with H.E., and offering statements admitting of
complete misunderstanding which made a journalist's holiday.
English friends were annoyed. He wrote her several letters
remonstrating about this (she did not keep any of these letters,
for she was inclined to treasure only those letters from
him in which there was no criticism of herself). She replied
with great irritation, saying—"You have hurt me badly." He
let it drop, and the cloud passed, for so long as she could be
the "hurt" person, she was content. The tour came to an
end, and she returned to England before the 1914-18 War
broke out, in high spirits and excellent health.

In a few months the War did break out. Its effect upon H.E.
can be most clearly discerned in his *Impressions and Comments*, Volume II. From his entry for August 14th, 1914—
"Today, it is said, five nations are beginning to fight the
greatest battle in the history of the world, and over the whole
cradle of human civilization the Powers of Hell are let loose.
Vae victis! Vae victoribus!" To the end it is always at the
back of his mind. He did not write very much about it in the
Impressions. But he lived in no ivory tower. "My bells are
jangled and fall silent," he wrote on October 19th, 1914. "I

am sorry. Yet I would not have it otherwise. They are not hung in an ivory tower." Feeling at that time that he would not bring reference to the war into his entries, though in the event this is not by any means true, he continued:

By day and by night I think of the Great War. But I never have any wish to write about it. If I could I would forget it. In the Peninsula War, it is said, one of Wellington's generals was guilty of a flagrant act of insubordination, and Wellington, who in little matters was so hard a disciplinarian, took no notice. They asked him later how it was. "By God," he replied, "it was too serious." This war today seems to me the most flagrant act of insubordination committed by Man against Civilization and Humanity. It is too serious for the lash of discipline to touch. We must leave it at that.

One volume of the *Impressions*, started in 1912, had already been written, and published in 1914. It was his habit to write several books at the same time. I think we may say that H.E. could claim some success in the art of living; and some success in the art of writing; but what I feel inclined to emphasize is his success in the art of getting his books written, and keeping about four entirely different sorts of books going at the same time. To a person like myself who can only deal with one book at a time, becoming soaked in it and hardly capable of answering a letter, his capacity to organize his many works in this way is a little puzzling.

There are two volumes of his under the general title of *Essays in War Time*—one of them also known as *The Philosophy of Conflict*. One of these essays has always seemed to me the most remarkable he ever wrote. It is called "Europe." When his *Selected Essays* were brought out in the Everyman Library, I took very little part in the selection, though I was privileged to write the Introduction. But I did persuade H.E. to include, whatever else might be omitted, this essay on Europe—and the reader will find it there. It stirs me in the same way as great poetry does. The war is not mentioned. It is the phenomenon of Europe that we see, that unique growth (and we glimpse the fact that the war is a civil war). But the poet lifts us up into contemplation far beyond the ephemeral agony of the nations until we see life as a lyric of everlasting catastrophe and a lyric of everlasting joy. If we are asked— What has Havelock Ellis to say to us today? our reply must be: his is the *genius of perspective*. Thus it is a dateless message. We surrender to him. We rise. We climb to the exalted place. We absent ourselves from bias. For a few brief moments we also are visionaries entering into that region of the understanding where sorrow is turned into beauty and all tears are wiped away.

The essay which gives its title to the book, *The Philosophy of Conflict*, is directly concerned with both the militarist and pacificist arguments of the time, and also propounds his philosophy of life in the schematic sense. At that time there were apologists for war on the ground that conflict was good because it developed the noble virtues of courage and sacrifice; and there were apologists for pacificism on the ground that all conflict is bad. "On the other side can we see the slightest recognition of that fundamental truth, built into the very foundations of life, of the universe itself, that conflict is a genus of many species, of which war is only one." This is H.E.'s Philosophy of Conflict—his reconciliation of Heaven and Hell. He conceives life as held together by opposing forces in harmonious action. The most obvious prototype of this is in architecture where we see the device of the arch in which two opposing forces each supports the other, and stability is insured. We see it in botany where "every unfolding frond of fern bears witness to a similar opposition of forces. Opposition is not a hindrance to life, it is a necessary condition for the becoming of life." We see it in dancing where the tension of opposing muscular action results in harmonious balance. We are faced with a general law of nature, more important than the laws of lawyers, comforting to understand and advisable to obey. War may at an earlier period have played its part in fruitful struggle, while in any case a primitive war lasting three years with a total of six deaths is rather more pleasing than a modern war lasting four years with a total of six million deaths, just as the exhortation to "increase and multiply" given to a people who consisted of eight persons, was more to the point than if announced to a people consisting of fifty millions.

H.E. was optimistic about the disappearance of war in the near future. He added up the causes why it should decay, chief of which he rated a falling birth-rate and an industrialism which had passed its climax. He lived long enough to witness the outbreak of the last war. His optimism was ill-founded. If he were alive today, would he be cheerful regarding the outlook? I think so. The conditions for dropping war really are present now. Wars, until this era, have generally been fought for land, or slaves, or gold, or oil, or uranium. But today—at any rate tomorrow—we have Zeta. If soon all the power needed can be got out of a glass of sea-water, then the old causes for war vanish. Are there new causes? There is the desire of the Communists to dominate the world? There may be that desire, and it may possibly be a powerful one. But it is nullified by the existence of the H-bomb. This is a happy moment in the history of mankind. We can all relax now with solid ground for optimism. At last we have the thing we have been waiting for, a shield against war. That shield might be used by some nation as a weapon. But that is a risk we must become accustomed to living under, and as the years pass we will become accustomed to it, while in the course of time the nations may be expected to work out the best means of living together more or less amicably. It would be amoral to cast aside the shield so that others might then with advantage use it as a weapon. True, there are some amongst us today, and they cannot strictly be called militarists, who would have us commit this wrong and outlaw, not war, but the *nuclear shield* against war! But I do not think they are a powerful enough body to make war inevitable.

I wrote above that I thought H.E. would share the cheerful outlook which many of us feel in this matter. I have, of course, been rereading most of his books. It happened that not long after I had written these remarks in a first draft, I came in my reading to the Third Volume of *Impressions and Comments*. There I found an entry which I had completely forgotten after reading it, as I suppose I did, years ago—it was then an Impression which made no impression on me. It makes rather pertinent reading for us today. I do not quote it with any hope of winning adherents to this view. This is a Debate in which no one listens to the other side: in fact those taking the other side are ruffians with a thoroughly amoral outlook—I see I have taken that line myself. Still, let us have the quotation, from February 8th, 1921.

A great engineering authority, Lord Headley, in his presidential address to the Society of Engineers yesterday, stated that immense progress is still possible in the practice of warfare, especially if we are ever able to harness the electrons. He foresaw a time when a general officer, sitting comfortably at his desk, might touch a button which would release destructive agencies capable of sweeping hundreds of square miles and annihilating the armies of the enemy, together with all other living things, while his own armies were similarly annihilated by the general officer in command on the other side similarly touching a button.

H.E. then suggests that it might be difficult to know what device should be adopted to enable the expectant nations to know which side had been victorious, since under the circumstances neither side would then exist (though I think this is an exaggeration). He continues:

But, however that may be decided, it should be Mankind's unceasing prayer that the day may come swiftly, for it is essential that war should be brought to an end. Men have dreamed of various ways in which the prayer might be answered. Some have believed that the end might be gained by the growth of the instinct of Sympathy. Some have believed in the growing influence of Reason. But we see that human emotion is remarkably one-sided in its action, and as to Reason, it plays a very subordinated part in the mental processes even of the Superior Persons whom our democracies set up to rule the world. Until the time when the conquest of the birth-rate has become so firmly established that human cannon fodder is too dear to use, the method foreseen by Lord Headley seems alone to hold out hope for Mankind. One might have preferred other less radical methods of attaining the same end. But evidently it was not to be.

22

I T WAS also at this time that he wrote his chapter on England as a start for his book on *The Genius of Europe*. It
was one of those many volumes for which he kept accumulating material throughout his life, and it was a task that he
very much wanted to carry out. It remained uncompleted.
Nevertheless a book with that title by H.E. was published by
an American firm[1] in 1951, consisting of the work he had done
—including, besides the essay on England, essays on the Genius of Russia, the Genius of France, the Genius of Spain, and
the Genius of Germany.

He regretted the destruction of the unity which at one time
held France and England together. A specialist in races, in the
significance and operations of blood-mixture and heredity,
H.E. could see nothing but disaster in that France should have
freed herself from the domination of the Normans who were
seeking to preserve her racial and prehistoric unity with England. He held that the Normans with their northern race and
southern civilization furnished a bond of union, equally
honourable both to France and to England, which it only
required the growth of tradition to develop. The "British
Isles" he points out, or rather reminds us, since we know it
only too well, is far from being a unity: it would have been
much more so if we had not been cut off from France. Thus,
as an instance of the first importance, he stresses the sympathy

[1] Rinehart & Company, New York.

of the Mediterranean population of France and the Mediterranean population of Ireland (for such it largely is, and the name De Valera does little to contradict it), and holds that such unity "would have forever rendered impossible an 'Irish Question.' " He thought that the advantage of the union of France and England for the world generally would have been incalculable. The weakness of a civilization founded on a broad and human basis of reason, such as that of France, "is that it is ever too ready to recognize its own limits and to rest satisfied with an epigram in the face of human stupidity. If the humanizing civilization of France had been backed by the energy of England, and held in check by our stolidity and love of compromise, there would have been moulded for the world's civilization the most effective instrument that can be conceived."

I used to wonder exactly why Joan of Arc was made a saint. She was a soldier. It was bad that she should have been burnt as a witch but strange that her activities should qualify her as a saint. I have enjoyed as much as anyone parts of Shaw's famous play, including the Epilogue. But I never could make out why, in that Epilogue, when Joan asks—"Shall I come back?" they are all so *apologetic* in their negative and slink off shamefacedly. The dialogue would have been more Shavian if at least one of them had been offensive in his reply to the inspired soldier—for, indeed, what would have been the point of her coming back? Who would have gained? And I never could understand why she should have been entitled to say as the curtain falls—"When will the world be ready to receive thy saints? How long, Oh Lord, how long?" I am told that the reason why she can be called saint is a theological one; that the Church recanted and finally held that she did not listen to the voice of the devil, or to her own voice, but to the voice of God. In which case we are bound to say, without offense, that whether God was on the side of the big or the small battalions, he was certainly not on the side of Europe generally. I had long puzzled over Joan's sainthood and annoyed people by asking how it is that we all accept that

curtain-fall question of hers, when in 1951 I read for the
first time H.E. on Joan of Arc. My question does not puzzle
him. It does not occur to him. All he has to say is—"When the
peasant girl of Lorraine, with her hallucinations, galvanized
into action the nerveless arms of Charles, she inflicted a blow
on the progress of the modern world which, so far as can be
seen, has never been equalled."

His essay on England is an elaborate extension in detail of
an entry he made in Volume I of *Impressions and Comments:*

What a strange fate it is that made England! A little ledge of
beautiful land in the ocean, to draw and to keep all the men of
Europe who had the sea in their hearts and the wind in their
brains, daring children of Nature, greedy enough and romantic
enough to trust their fortunes to waves and to gales. The most
eccentric of peoples, all the world says, and the most acquisi-
tive, made to be pirates and made to be poets, a people that have
fastened their big teeth into every quarter of the globe and
flung their big hearts at the feet of Nature, and even done both
things at the same time. The man who wrote the most magnificent
sentence in the English language was a pirate and died on the
scaffold.[1]

It is the peculiar position of England as a one-time citadel
in the sea which has made the English so hard to understand,
since the very men who came to the land, the strong, the
practical, the dreamer-adventurous, were not even typical of
their first homeland. The Englishman is the outcome of a
unique process of selection, making him at once adventurer
and pirate no less than dreamer and poet, passionately devoted
to freedom to the verge of eccentricity, and not only a stern
moralist peculiarly apt for piety but an aggressive colonizer
and a hard-headed man of business. It is easy to see why such
a people could be eulogized on the one hand as patterns of
loyalty and honour, of moderation and stability, as champions
of the oppressed and upholders of freedom in the world, and

[1] Sir Walter Raleigh, of course.

also castigated as brutal and cruel and sullen affording the supreme examples of the hypocrite and the humbug. In pointing to the effect which the successive waves of invasion, Celtic, Anglo-Saxon, Scandinavian, Norman, each made in the formation of the strange amalgam we call British, H.E. passes in review the chief aspects of the nation's genius, practical, literary, religious, philosophic. Of English philosophers before they meekly decided that philosophy has nothing to do with life, he says—

The dreamer, the adventurer, the individualist, the iconoclast, the Puritan, stalks through the whole of English philosophy. It is the same, no matter whether we date that philosophy from Scotus Erigena or from the superb audacity and insight of the insolent friar, Roger Bacon. Francis Bacon, throwing aside the whole weighty tradition of antiquity with an exalted faith in Nature and in Practice; Hobbes, with his disdain for others and his absolute trust in his own good reason; Locke, with all the zeal of a Puritan, laying bare the *tabula rasa* of the mind; Berkeley, with delicate skill building up a dream world on the site of the material world he had destroyed; Hume, with his solvents to melt away all the venerated faiths of his time; William Godwin, the father of all philosophic anarchism; Thomas Paine, who inspired the ideas of the Constitution of the United States; Herbert Spencer, with his concentrated passion of hatred against every fetter that society seeks to bind on the freedom of the individual; John Stuart Mill, who elevated and enlarged the English conception of individualism to become a rampart against the levelling influence of democracy as much as against the crushing influence of autocracy, who sought to bring women within its circle on the same terms as men, and pointed the way to the conclusion that, rightly understood, there is no real conflict between individualism and socialism—all these were daring and high-souled pioneers who left the old world behind them and steered to new and unknown shores. And the new horizons they revealed have enlarged the scope of the world for all mankind.

It may be doubted whether any thinker previous to H.E. has been so interested in tracing how blood comes out in spirit, or who held as firmly to the belief that the subtlest variations of a man's outlook on the world are determined centuries before he is born. It is illuminating to see Shakespeare focused in this beam.

It would be surprising if Shakespeare, the supreme glory of English literature, were an exception to the rule that English art is the exact reflection of the complex racial elements that make up the English people and the English spirit. In Shakespeare the west and the east, the Celt and the Anglo-Saxon, were fused together with unique and scarcely analysable felicity. Warwickshire is not only, as has often been pointed out, the heart of England, it also represents anthropologically an infolding of the darker people of the west among the fairer Angles, and is thus an admirable centre for a slow and complete process of racial mixture. In surveying Shakespeare's work we may indeed be inclined to think that its Celtic qualities outweigh the Anglo-Saxon. All this vivacity and quick wit, this vivid perception of the sensory aspects of the world, this gay extravagance, this art of weaving a brilliant and variegated tapestry of words, all this is Celtic. Here we are in the world of Cuchullainn and the *Mabinogion*. Yet even when Shakespeare is most Celtic he is still also Anglo-Saxon. From this point of view Mercutio and Falstaff are technically interesting, for here we see the Celtic spirit with delightful effect playing through solid fleshy Anglo-Saxon figures. But such figures are merely the byplay of Shakespeare's composite genius. The Anglo-Saxon in him is really fundamental; he is Norse, even Norman, in his oligarchic sympathies, in his fundamental instinct for personal independence and personal responsibility, in the profound melancholy from which his gaiety exhales. In his most visionary outlook he is still on the solid ground of human emotion at its most poignant degree of concentrated intensity. It is from the sharp conflict, the explosive union, of these two elements of the west and of the east, that the flaming splendour of *Lear* proceeds. We may even say that the Anglo-Saxon spirit is the primary element in Shakespeare's character, for we seem to find it almost unmixed in the youthful *Venus and Adonis*, even in the Sonnets, while the Celtic spirit was never more prominent than at the end of his life in *The Tempest*. It is by the vital opposition of these two conflicting elements in the English nation, by the magnificent effect which their fusion may yield, that Shakespeare is in the end so absolutely English. No Englishman in real life ever fully embodied the characteristics of Shakespeare; yet Shakespeare is all England.

H.E. wrote this essay on England in 1916 at Speen in the Chiltern Hills. Edith had made one of her impulsive "finds" which were by no means always unsuccessful. This was a little paradise of a place where they spent a happy summer near beech woods in which they could wander without meeting a soul, and they had a delightful garden. He says he wrote this long essay (among other things) without effort, animated, he tells us, by a patriotic enthusiasm aroused by the war, which he had never felt before—"I may add that I have never felt it since." He may have thought that he was too laudatory. It is certainly possible to feel that England's vitality may have run down, and that the mixture is no longer fermenting. True, the women are now going very strong— but a great many of her best men were lost by the two last wars. It may be suggested that such a view was disproved by the spirit of the people during the last war. It is true that the Englishman springs to life under catastrophe when all the fine qualities come out like plants after rains. But it has to be the kind of catastrophe which he can enjoy dramatically. In the future there may not be enough of this kind to go round.

H.E. never wavered in his love for France, Spain, and Russia, and I could as fruitfully have quoted from his essays on those countries—and am very sorry to leave out his set piece on Tolstoy. He did not care for Germany so much, but the same broad sympathy is evident, the same knowledge of the social, literary, scientific, and philosophic fields over which he moves elsewhere. I have high hopes that Havelock Ellis will never become compulsory reading in schools or universities. Thus it may always be open to anyone in his twenties or his thirties or his forties or later, who has a fancy for education, to take him up and enjoy an unexpected experience.

23

MEANWHILE his matrimonial life continued on the uneven tenor of its way. For, having piled up more debts, Edith decided upon a second visit to the United States. He did not dissuade her, for the debts were excessive and beyond his control. She had been successful before, and there was no reason why she should not be again. And sure enough, when she arrived she met once more with the wonderful American politeness and hospitality which have gladdened so many hearts from the Old World. And, we must remember, her own nature called out love. "I shall always see her as she was here at first," an American woman wrote to H.E. years later, "so interested in everybody and everything, and herself so interesting, and her beautiful nature, so warm and kind she was." But her health was far from equal to the strain. She needed his support. She continually pleaded with him to come out. America would give him such a welcome. But on this he always did take a strong line. He could not do it. It would be impossible for him. It would be torture. "It is not possible for me to come out" he wrote to her, "but even if it were possible I fear I should be a worry to you and I should certainly be wretched. I shall rejoice to see you again, but you must not feel homesick or come back before you are quite ready. If you were here now I really do not quite know what we should do, without money and with no Rose Cottage; London is not very attractive, even in an ordinary win-

ter," etc. In the years to come he brooded over this, knowing
that though he would not go to her, she would never have
failed to come to him if he called upon her at any time. For
again he writes—"I am always thinking of you with love. I
shall rejoice to see you again, but am not specially anxious
you should come back in the bad weather or into the gloom
of war, and of course shall be glad if you can fulfil your
purpose and make money." The fact is their independent basis
on the financial aspect in marriage meant that he could never
control the situation with prudent planning according to
means, and when she ran disastrously into debt he was unable
to meet the bill. And now he was glad that she was out of
the way in America making some money to pay her debts.
(These debts must have been considerable for she had written
to him from the *Olympic*, which at one time was in danger
of U-boat attack, "I never felt so horrible in all my life as
when I felt I might leave you with all those debts to face.")

Meanwhile, in spite of her somewhat overwrought and
nervous condition, she went ahead with her lectures on "Sex
and Eugenics" and "Sane Eugenics with a Fine Spirituality"
and "The Loves of Tomorrow" and kindred titles. Her remarkable voice and personal address carried the day, but the
general excitement increased her neurotic tendencies, and
though she was making money she felt that she could not
afford to spend what she ought on food to keep her going—
"a sixpenny breakfast here costs a dollar!" Nevertheless during all the whirl of excitement and strain and confusion she
wrote him letter after letter of love and solicitude. This suddenly changed to resentment.

It was his fault. During this winter he had been
living in retirement and loneliness at his Brixton flat. One day
an American woman called on him. He had not previously
heard of her though she was well known in America—Mar-
garet Sanger. His books had been an inspiration to her and
now she formed a favourable impression of the author.
They became friends. They were happy and at ease in one
another's company. She was an American of Irish origin. He

was not the first man, nor the last, to find that combination irresistible. They never jarred on each other. He had never known a more genial or charming companion—and it was the swiftest friendship he had ever made. The relationship was what is called "innocent." He says it was one of calm friendship "even though there was a sweet touch of intimacy about it"; and in parenthesis he adds, revealingly—"I speak more especially concerning my own attitude in it, and she showed herself beautifully willing to accept my attitude." For him there was no trace of guilty consciousness to spoil it. No sooner was he sure of this new friendship than he proceeded to tell his wife all about it! In letter after letter he sang her praises. It did not occur to him that this would come as in any sense a shock to her, since, as a regular thing she herself was constantly forming new friendships. It is strange that he did not think it unwise to tell her about it. Once again we appear to be faced with the fact that H.E. was lacking in knowledge of women in some important respects. He did not take into account the unbooked laws of feminine reaction. A woman will say—"Do take care of yourself while I am away, and enjoy yourself. Why don't you take X out and have a lovely time." This must not be taken seriously. A woman will say— "I don't mind if you have an affair with some one, it wouldn't worry me a bit." Yet woe to the man who takes this seriously and says—"Well, as a matter of fact I have been intimate with some one." For the woman will instantly change. She may even become quite paralysed with horror, go quiet and dead, and even after years the damage done may never be repaired. I suppose this is a universal fact. But what man credits it until he has actually experienced it? Certainly not the open, entirely undeceitful H.E.

It is bad enough when this happens in a verbal exchange. On this occasion the harm was done in a series of letters, and weeks had to pass before he was to know the result of his first letter. Being so sure of her he failed to realize that she was never sure of herself, and therefore of him. Her natural vein of suspicion and self-distrust caused the contents of his letters to produce an earthquake in her heart. He was surprised at this. (He was surprised also that Amy was indignant.) His first letter arrived just after she had posted a newspaper cutting to him in which she was quoted as talking about "loving the woman one's man loves." She herself felt this to be slightly ironic—I would call it poetic justice. She would not upbraid him, she wrote. She was not jealous, only stunned. It was merely that she wished she could die. It was more than she could bear. The wound in her heart was deep. And so on through many long letters, at the close of one of which she says—"I have no heart or strength to write long letters. You see you don't see *what* I mean. It is not you have ceased to care—it is—well, just what it is, and perhaps only a woman knows what that is . . ." Her letters should not damage her in our eyes. She quotes Wilde's remark that each man kills the thing he loves. Certainly each man kills the thing that loves him. Subsequently he discovers that he needs the love that he has killed—and finds that it is *no longer there*. This tragedy is known more to men than to women.

But generalizations do not always apply. This does not apply here. It might have been a good thing if H.E. had carried out a swift offensive and written to her in brief anger. He did not do so. He wrote patiently. He remained calm. He quotes a letter of his and comments—"It is a simple letter and calm, perhaps too calm in face of her pain and agitation. But it had become my part in life always to remain calm in face of her agitation and so to seek to soothe her pain, knowing that that pain was likely to pass swiftly away." She was nearly always agitated, on the grade up or on the grade down. And she was often ill, though quickly recovering. The difficulty about such people is that in the end no one takes their illnesses seriously, expecting quick recuperation. The time comes when they really are ill. It was so now. She had over-strained herself. Her strength was undermined by disease. He did not realize this. She was obliged to give up her engagements and had only just enough energy to board a very crowded Amer-

ican liner (the *Lusitania* had just been sunk) and sail home
in great discomfort.

He met her at Liverpool. She picked up on meeting him
again. He felt reassured as to the state of her health in body
and mind. But when they reached Brixton he was soon to re-
vise this opinion. Amy called one day. He left them alone for
a little, and Amy made some remarks, "not happily inspired"
about his care and kindness which would soon help her to get
strong again. When H.E. was showing Amy to the door,
Edith swallowed a number of morphia tablets. He comments,
"The act was unpremeditated, inconsequential, a child's act.
She quietly told me at once what she had done: she meekly
swallowed the simple emetic I hastened to prepare; the tablets
were speedily returned and no ill results followed." He now
realized the extent to which her mind and body had been
weakened, for this was the first time she had given evidence
of suicidal thoughts, to say nothing of suicidal attempts.

They went to spend the summer again at Speen in the
Chilterns, where they had been so happy before. Naturally
that happiness was not to be repeated. She now became easily
exhausted. In earlier days when she was tired and irritable
she would quickly recover after a good dinner and some wine.
Now there was no such recuperation, she would sit in a dejection out of which he could not move her, and she would
bring up her grievances which no argument could dislodge.
At night her melancholy reached its worst, and one early
morning she went quietly to the well just outside the house
with the intention of throwing herself down it, though at
the last moment had not the courage to do so.

Soon her woman friend of that period came down to Speen.
This gave him a break and he went to London. But she
wrote to him in a melancholy strain. Her friend had found a
new friend and talked of her all day instead of ministering to
Edith. The latter now feels she is a "mere incumbrance"; she
is very ill but cannot die. Nevertheless as the months passed
her spirits began to revive. She planned another visit to the

United States. And once again she implored him to accompany her. There had been a good deal of gossip about them in New York and rumours that they were not properly married. She wanted to produce her husband and show that her license was in perfect order. She promised that she would protect him from the social life; and as an aid to this proposed that he should sit on the platform while she lectured on him. It was at this time that Jo Davidson, the sculptor, had just modelled his bust. When she saw the sculptor's vision of a tortured and anxious soul brooding in a contemplative sadness, she declared that it was not like him. "You have never seen him!" he retorted. A salutary remark—especially just then. Even so, whether she had seen him or not, her love for him is most touching. Whenever he was away at this time, even for a few days, she wrote to him, sometimes twice a day, letters which contain such depth of tenderness, letters written not so much by a woman as by a child, that it is easy to understand her hold upon his heart.

Had he been other than he was, he might have been made cold and cruel. He might have wearied. But he never wearied. He had entered now into nearly the last stage of this journey and he intended to endure to the end. Once again they were together in Cornwall. This old environment did something to restore her mental balance and she threw off her depression and suspicion, and seemed on the road to recovery. A new maid, Millie, had come to help her from London—for Priscilla had left her after a quarrel. But unable to stand Edith's changes of mood and bitter tongue, Millie left after an unrestrained scene, calling out as she went that she was very sorry for H.E.—a mark of sympathy which he "curtly repelled." This episode had a bad effect. She developed persecution mania. She imagined the neighbours were plotting against her; they were calling her a drunkard; they were planning to rob her—and she removed her pearls and some other treasure into the safe keeping of friends at St. Ives. She became the opposite to her former self. She no longer wanted to organize anything. She neglected the house. Her pride and her will left her, with her wilfulness, her independence, and her defiance. He would prepare a bath for her, and she would go to take it: half an hour later he would find her still standing beside it. She found it almost impossible to dress, since this involved deciding which garment to wear. She would sit in front of her food without eating it, or before a letter without writing it, or stop on the stairs and remain there for an indefinite period. At night, after he had tucked her up in bed, she was restless and continually called for him. Sometimes, worn out and weary, he would not hear her or fail to respond, but more often he would rise and go in and soothe her.

It will be seen that, in the exact meaning of the words, he rose to the occasion. Many of us fail to do this, allowing ourselves to become irritable or unkind. But nothing lasts for long, and the time comes when the trial is over, and the person perhaps is dead. Then we suffer remorse. Why were we not kinder? why not more patient?—and now that it is too late we look back in anguish. If only we could have a second chance. "Is your present experience hard to bear?" wrote Edward Carpenter in one of his many striking pieces in *Towards Democracy*. "Yet remember that never again perhaps in all your days will you have another chance of the same. Do not fly the lesson, but have a care that you master it while you have the opportunity." Those Christians who are pained at the absence of doctrinal belief in the position of Havelock Ellis may note his *active* participation in the central value of Christianity. Years earlier he had made a translation of the fifth book of *The Imitation of Christ*, which he conceived to be as deep and true a statement of the meaning of love as was ever written down. He gave that sheet of translation to his wife before their marriage. She carried it with her always and cherished it to the last. It was now his chance to learn the full truth of the words written long ago by the strangely inspired mediaeval monk: "A great thing is love, a great and altogether a good thing; for love alone makes every heavy burden light, and every unequal burden equal. Because it bears the burden without being burdened, and makes every bitter thing sweet and delicious. Like the living and ardent flame of a torch it ever rises and safely passes through all." H.E. never had to look back in remorse about this time. She relied entirely upon him. He never failed her. It did not affect his health. "Such, then, is the power of love that I seemed none the worse for the constant strain. . . . My service was accepted and my love was answered. That makes all the difference in the world, even to physical health." His service was accepted and his love was answered—that was the important thing.

But it was clear that neither she nor he could continue like this much longer without help from outside. She was mentally as well as physically ill, as is obvious to anyone at all familiar with these things, such as her inability to rouse herself, her sitting on the stairs or standing before the bath without the will to move. A doctor and friends managed, with inevitable difficulty, to persuade her to go into a Convent Nursing Home at Hayle. There she was to be excluded from her world, seeing no one save H.E., who took rooms a few minutes' walk away. He then entered into the last phase, of which he says, "Now began a period during which I was tortured as I have never before or since been tortured for so long in my life. I was outwardly calm; then and since I confided to no one; yet even today, when all is receding into the past, when nothing matters, it is only with an effort of resolution that I force myself to write of those weeks."

The facts can be briefly set down. At first she appeared to be improving. To forward this it occurred to H.E. that it would be a good thing to ask her woman friend of that period to send her some flowers and fruit. This was done but with bad results. An hour later she managed to elude the nurses and throw herself from the lavatory window. She injured her foot, cut her head, and lay in bed for some days unconscious.

It was never understood why this token of affection had such an influence for evil. It changed the course of her illness. The melancholy that had clung to her for months was dissipated by the shock. But this was only superficially beneficial, for the Mother Superior was alarmed and anxious to get rid of her, and she was transferred to a Nursing Home in London for mental cases, which happened to be conveniently close to his Brixton flat, where she settled in quite happily, and her old energy began to be restored. But it took a wrong turn. An American friend called and got on with her so well that Edith was flattered and invited her to stay the night. This was against the rules of the Home and the Superintendent being away, the nurses could not sanction it. Edith was furious and decided to leave next morning. She now began to adopt an attitude of ostentatious independence towards H.E. Exchanging her mood of morbid apathy for morbid energy she carried away all her baggage from the Brixton flat and visited various friends at a maximum of discomfort to herself and to them. She then went off to Cornwall without a word to him, taking with her an orphaned youth she had met on a bus, called him her adopted son, and lavished upon him gifts and clothes without possessing the funds to do so. He repaid her with indifference and later went to prison. In so far as she visited Cornwall with the intention of exhibiting her mental and physical recovery and normality to her friends, it is strange that she should have produced this youth as an aid in this endeavour. In any case it was doomed to failure for all sorts of rumours had preceded her and she was received with reserve and caution and prevented from going near their children as she might be "dangerous." She heard that she was to be shut up in an asylum, papers having already been signed to that effect by her husband. She hastened back to London and decided, to the surprise and scorn of the charming youth whom she still had with her, to go to H.E. He was not at home. He had gone away for a few days to Norfolk.

This was unfortunate. Had he been there to greet her (though how he would have coped with the youth is a scene difficult to visualize) the high comedy of the last phase might have been less tragic. She had accepted seriously the rumour that he had proposed to get her shut up, and she felt that now she could not trust him. The only way to safeguard herself, she thought, was to get a legal separation, so that his writ could not operate. She told him that if only he hadn't betrayed her but had given her his care and devotion she would have pulled through, and nothing could make her see that this was exactly what he had done as well as carefully avoiding the certificate. The Contract of Separation was drawn up and delivered to him by her lawyer. He accepted it. He knew that her motive for drawing it up was because she believed that he was a menace to her personal freedom, and he thought she would feel better when she had secured this "separation." He was glad and sad at the same time. The essence of the Deed of Separation was that he should set forth that she "may at all times hereafter live separate and apart as if she were unmarried" and that he should not "for any purpose whatsoever use force or restraint to her person or liberty." There was also a clause which she put in equally creditable to her and pleasing to him—namely, that she would indemnify him against all debts and at all times keep and maintain herself. They went together with this strange document to the Law Society in Fetter Lane and signed it in the presence of two grave lawyers, after which they had lunch together in an amicable state of mind. It only remained for him to assist her in setting up a new flat. It was rather an expensive one, and she persuaded him to accompany her round to agents and upholsterers, her motive, which at the time he failed to detect, being that the presence of a husband is a guarantee in such business arrangements. In this flat she had a special room, next to her own, fitted up as a bedroom for himself. He refused to use it. It seemed to him "a little ridiculous" that a man whose wife had just arranged a legal separation should share rooms with her. He knew that she needed him near her at night as she had needed him before and as he had administered to her before. He did not come. Various friends took his place. She turned the room into a "lecture hall" with a little platform, in which she gave frequent lectures and readings to an audience of six on the Superman, the Future of

Civilization, the Place of Woman in Society, and The Loves of Tomorrow. She pleaded with him to come and "take the chair" in order to demonstrate that they were not really separated. He did not do so. He told her that he could not break his life-long rule of never, under any circumstances whatever, making "a public appearance."

She now assumed what at first appeared to be her normal self. She was full of schemes and new ideas, all promising tremendously well for the future—"I'm full of adventures and there is no doubt whatever about the future—none." Since many of her schemes were difficult to follow she commanded a following, though to her real friends it became clear that she was dying. She increased the number of lectures in the spare room to a daily performance. She hired halls. She employed two secretaries. She founded a publishing business in her flat, called it the Shamrock Press and commissioned a firm of printers to do a new edition of her book *My Cornish Neighbours*, and proposed to print a pamphlet by Marie Corelli, taking a taxi from London to Stratford-on-Avon to meet the novelist (the hire of the cab for this journey, together with other long ones, being paid by H.E. after her death). She started to promote a film company for the production of films that would raise the level of the screen. She planned to take the Little Theatre in Chicago for the winter season to further her dramatic interests. She undertook research for a book on Swedenborg, for which purpose she wished to obtain the use of a private room in the British Museum for the convenience of one of her secretaries. She supported the cause and propagated the aims of the Sufi movement led by Imayat Khan.

When something brought in some money she borrowed more and spent it so recklessly that she was sometimes actually penniless and unable to obtain food. Meanwhile she occasionally met H.E. and exchanged letters with him, but both in her letters and at the meetings she brought up old grievances and made fantastic charges. She did not visit him alone, for she had been "warned" not to come alone, and it was only to wrangle. She would pour out accusations regarding his falsity of which she had "positive proof." He would endure it patiently rather in the manner in which he had endured the bully at school who had used him as a horse. He put up no defence. He said nothing. But it left him crushed. She had come with good intentions, not meaning to make a scene, but before long she could not help breaking out, and some little gift, a bunch of grapes perhaps, which he had got for her would be forgotten and she would leave without it. But she did not believe that he had been silent and endured the accusations with scarce a word. One day after she had been particularly truculent, the friend reproached her as they were going home for some of the bitter things she had said. "But think of the things he said to me!" was her reply. He might just as well have said them.

In early September of this year, 1916, the first Zeppelin was brought down in flames to the north of London. The spectacle could be clearly seen from where she was living. There was a good deal of alarm in the district. She was not alarmed. She wanted to see the sight and went out to join a group of people in the street, with no more than a cloak thrown over her pyjamas. A woman in the group complained of the cold, and Edith took off her own cloak and placed it round the woman. This brought on a chill, and she was unable to keep an appointment to meet H.E. for lunch. He called on her and found her in bed with a nurse by her side. She was bright and cheerful, already recovering from what was thought to be an attack of pleurisy. She assured him that she would soon be well, and urged him to go, as he happened to have planned, for a day or so to Suffolk with his old friend Barker Smith. He was a little doubtful about this but it seemed safe, for on the Monday he got a message from the nurse saying that she was sure to be well in a few days, and he set out and received on the Tuesday a second reassuring note. He decided not to return till the Wednesday. Reaching his flat on that day he found a telegram waiting for him—"Mrs. Ellis dying. Come at once."

The cheerfulness and sudden flame of vitality which she had displayed on the Monday was illusory, it was really the approach of death. On the Tuesday there had come a swift change for the worse. A veil of coma spread over her consciousness. It seems that she could recognize those around her a little, and made an effort to convey to the nurse a wish that H.E. should be sent for, by pointing to his photograph on the wall—but the nurse did not understand her. When he did arrive she was still alive, with eight hours more to go, but she had now lost the power of speech or recognition. Nurses and doctors and friends had been by her bedside in constant attention. The Deed of Separation had caused the absence of her husband. Thus she died without knowing that he was beside her.

She was at peace at last. And he also was at peace. "We are glad even when those we are fond of die," said Bernard Shaw, "for we have finally got them out of the way." That is a very Irish manner of expressing grief. The English do not take kindly to such a remark: I remember Middelton Murry telling me how much some of Shaw's remarks pained him. Still, it is a good thing to be oneself even at the risk of being thought too light-handed. It is also a good thing to be oneself even at the risk of being thought too heavy-handed. H.E. puts it this way:

Grief is one of the greatest mysteries of life. In losing a beloved person one is plunged into sorrow. Yet at the same time one is raised above all doubts and fears and anxieties into a sphere of joy which nothing can henceforth touch. While the loved one lived there is always doubt whether the love will last; there is always fear of giving or receiving hurt; there is always apprehension of harm to the being who is so dear. Now one is raised forever above all doubt and fear and anxiety. One enters the heaven of complete and eternal possession which nothing can henceforth touch. To think of the loved one is now of all pleasures the greatest. What one truly loves is veritably one's own soul, and to lose one's soul, as religion makes clear, is to gain it, for love is, in a certain sense, religion. All the ardours of religious love—even its saints and its relics and its shrines and its Holy Places—are but the transformations of the simple facts of natural love.

My narrative of his life closes here, for I have sought to deal only with his most fruitful and creative years, making no more claim now at the end than at the beginning to write an exhaustive biography. In fact he had twenty-three years to live. I think they were the happiest years of his life—though they brought more personal problems to be overcome.[1] They were spent with Françoise Delisle,[2] and it was through her that he spent his declining years where he most desired to be, in Suffolk, the home of so many of his ancestors. Françoise is still with us, and has fortified me in the preparation of this book, rejoicing in his memory as he rejoiced in her.

[1] See *Friendship's Odyssey* by Françoise Delisle.
[2] Amy married circa 1919.

24

I COULD not have written this narrative without H.E.'s *My Life*. A true autobiography, as opposed to memories and memoirs, ought to deal with the man's inner development as well as his outward circumstance. I used to wish that Shaw, in his old age, instead of writing those bad plays, had written an autobiography. It would have been marvellously good fun. The comic muse would have played upon all the outer circumstances, including galleries of extraordinary persons, but of himself and his inner life and growth he would have revealed almost nothing. He would never have worn his heart, or his mind, upon his sleeve—though this is just what the truly great should do for us. Now, to Havelock Ellis, who was never led astray by the comic muse since he was never visited by it, there was "outside the limits of imaginative art, no form so precious in its nature and so permanent in its value as autobiography." He held the view that, adequately rendered, the pilgrim's progress of the soul through life should be as noble a record as Bunyan's, and more instructive; yet he thought that nearly all the "lives" written in his time were false or unprofitable. Passing in review the whole range of autobiography, he thought that only the *Confessions* of Rousseau, the *Confessions* of St. Augustine, and the *Memoirs* of Casanova could be placed at the summit. I believe he thought that he could succeed as well as they. But he knew that he could not possibly take any of them as a model. "The very qualities, indeed, of sanity and reasonableness, of critical impartiality, of just analytic precision, which made the task fascinating and possible for me, were incompatible with those qualities which had assured the success of Rousseau and Augustine and Casanova"—Rousseau stimulated by the torture of his need for self-justification, Augustine by his self-abandonment to religious emotion, Casanova by "a certain audacious moral obtusity." He knew that he could apply the scientific attitude to life, the living person: this was not impossible for him, if he could find a way compatible with the prudery and prejudices of his age. I think he was satisfied that he had found a way. He regarded this task as "the chief work" of his life—so he says indeed. He wrote *My Life* over a long period of years, setting aside the most propitious hours for its composition, on certain definite days, in the open air, chiefly in Cornwall. What did he do it for? Not to score off anyone; not for vanity; not for glory; not for pecuniary gain: he could enjoy nothing of these things since the book would not be published in his lifetime. He admits that it was partly the sheer instinct of the artist to use this material, and because of the desire that he might help others who should come after him to live their own lives.

It scarcely succeeds as a work of art. It is not equally inspired throughout. It even lacks economy in places. The first thirty pages are devoted to his ancestry. This has put off many readers. I myself tend to skip till he reaches his mother and father—though I love the first page with its evocation of sailing ships. The fact is he was a specialist in heredity and genealogy and ancestral influence; this flair enters into very many of his works, and he could not refrain from giving himself the full treatment. After page thirty I do not feel like skipping a word for some two hundred pages. He narrates the outward events while his emphasis is upon the growth of the poet's mind and the opening of the buds. This is not delightful. It is not good fun. It is interesting: it is what we need in a true autobiography. After this it must be admitted that, to a certain extent only, the work becomes bogged down by his wife. We understand his aim: to paint a full portrait of himself and her, letters and all. He thought it would be helpful to fully portray two human beings coming together, and to show how all human beings, gifted or commonplace, are much the same in essentials when facing marriage as when facing death or danger or other levellers. He thought it might help others if he presented the full picture, not omitting childishness in sentiment and phraseology, for of course in this region there is much childishness in the sense that grown-up people of both sexes feel the need to be mothered rather more than children do, and even to indulge in baby-talk rather more than babies. If we are prepared to take this from Swift in his *Letters to Stella* we might take it from H.E. (I'm not sure that I will take it from anyone else.)

My Life cannot be called a great work of art, nor even a wholly successful presentation of a man. But it is a rewarding work, and we are bound to feel it as such and be rewarded if we are prepared to surrender to his rhythm and read slowly, as he himself advanced slowly with great elephantine treads, and grew slowly and surely with the massive certainty of a tree. If a man writes to a rhythm—and no man touches the fringe of literature who does not write to a rhythm—he is difficult to read by anyone unable to flow at that pace or in that way, though the same reader may be perfectly happy with quite stiff books written with no style and no rhythm. It would be inconceivable that there could be any excessive or loud response to such a book as *My Life*. It can only be prized, be revered, by the reader who surrenders to the rhythm and the message and the man. It occurred to me the other day for the first time what was meant in the Bible by the exhortation to *believe* in Christ: "he that believeth in me shall not perish but have everlasting life." We must believe in the gods if we are to understand the gods, to enter into their blessedness and to bathe in their glory. It is wonderful how much we can get out of a man if we decide to think him good. Far more may be got out of him than is there, you may say. Yes indeed. Once *carte blanche* is given to the learned and the clever and, for that matter, the stupid, to praise, the results are sometimes remarkable. It is often seen. We have seen much of it in relation to D. H. Lawrence: no doubt he had, and still has, much to give. I think a little can also be found in Havelock Ellis. What is the chief thing about his autobiography? It is this: that here is a man who is *wearing no mask*. He is absolutely natural. He is concerned with the truth. With a kind of divine contempt he is indifferent to any charge of weakness or hardness, of modesty or immodesty, or anything else. There is no disguise here, nor deceit, nor humbug, nor hypocrisy, nor anything of the playboy. This is rather rare. He wore no mask; he put on no act; he created no legend; he encouraged no myth; he preached no religion; he raved not, neither did he rant. His reward is great. He has been spared by the sycophants of the saviours. He has never become the victim of doctrinaires. No one has borne false witness against his name. He has not been hailed in the market place as a prophet. And so, when he comes before us, nothing stands in our way: we can actually discern his features and hear his words.

25

IN HIS Autobiography, while being careful to start with and to carry out during the winding-up process, an account of his mental as well as his emotional development, he fails to do this throughout the whole book; he does not succeed in mentioning the production of all his chief publications —even omitting to say that *Affirmations* was published in 1892 when he was at Hawkes Point. It is a little lame, and even an admission of technical defeat, for an autobiographer to say, after a long and exhausting account of troubles with his wife that he does not wish to suggest that any of this was visible to the outsider or "interfered with the general course of my literary and other activities in the world. I may say indeed that I had never been more busily occupied than I was at this time, nor do I think that at any time my work was of better quality." He mentions the writing of *The Dance of Life* and other books and then goes back to his story.

I was unwilling to break up my own brief chronicle of that drama, but am now free to mention *The Dance of Life*, published in 1923. It has been widely read. He tells how it was the first book which brought him in some money. In America "it became a recognized best-seller, a unique experience for any book of mine. For one half-year the royalty that reached me amounted to £1,000." He used to reflect with some bitterness that while his reputation was going round the world he yet found it difficult to pay his way. We know how today an elaborate Study or Report on the subject of Sex easily becomes a best-seller. It was H.E. who made that possible. He made money for others but could not for himself, just as he could save others in the field of sex but not himself. But no true artist hopes or seeks salvation for himself: he is content [*au fond*] if he somehow gets the work done, though the getting of it done may leave him marred.

The Dance of Life is one of the bigger branches of this tree. Once again he leads us to a high place. When we look down from a height we see natural phenomena spread before us—the waters, the lands, the plants, the animals. We can contemplate the scene calmly, without fear or anxiety or prejudgment or attachment. We see that life takes this form and that form and the other form, and we rejoice to behold the Diversity. We see more than that from our hill: we see the life of man. We see it flowing in this direction and that direction, we see this growth and that growth, the Chinese or the Lifuanian, the Red Indians or the British; we see the Heroes of Man as saviour or sage, as soldier or scientist, as worshipper or poet. And because we look from a great height, because we are not involved or anxious or fearful, we will not fall into a dogmatic, judging, moral attitude of mind, but rather behold all these forms as different expressions of a fundamental substance. When we look at life in this liberated way, H.E. claims, what we find is easy to sum up. "We find, that is to say, that Man has forced himself to move along this line, and that line, and the other line. But it is the same water of life that runs in all these channels. Until we have ascended to a height where this is clear to see, all our little dogmatisms will but lead us astray." When we look at the world from this standpoint we do not say that here was the Chinese civilization and here the Lifuanian, one superior to the other, one perhaps good and the other bad (the latter ate each other sometimes, though with the highest motives): we rejoice to see the water of life flowing and sparkling in every direction.

If we do ascend this height we will agonize less about the world—and the paradox (if you care to call it so) is that, as Keats put it, "None can usurp this height save those to whom the agonies of the world are agonies and will not let them rest." Gazing from this view-point we will not find it necessary to be *only* ethical in our attitude. Thus there is the phenomenon known as Napoleon. H. G. Wells, in his *Outline of History*, roundly condemns him as a complete scoundrel. "There is no occasion to question this condemnation when we place ourselves in the channel along which Mr. Wells moves," says H.E., "it is probably inevitable; we may even accept it heartily. Yet, however right along that line, that is not the only line in which we may move. Moreover—and this is the point which concerns us—it is possible to enter a sphere in which no such merely negative, condemnatory, and dissatisfying a conclusion need be reached. For obviously it is dissatisfying. It is not finally acceptable that so supreme a protagonist of humanity, acclaimed by millions, of whom many gladly died for him, and still occupying so large and glorious a place in the human imagination, should be dismissed in the end as merely an unmitigated scoundrel. For so to condemn him is to condemn Man who made him what he was. He must have answered some lyric cry in the human heart."

Bertrand Russell in speaking about *The Dance of Life* in the volume published in America called *Havelock Ellis: In Appreciation*, contributed to by forty-four different hands on the occasion of his seventieth birthday, said—"The tragic facts of human life seem to have lost their sting for him, and to have been somehow harmonized as they are in tragic drama." He attained this standpoint, Russell holds, by virtue of his mystic experience. That is perfectly true; and indeed it has long been held that the spectator of tragic drama is lifted into a mystical acceptance of the world, and one recalls how Berlioz on witnessing *King Lear* fell into an ecstasy lasting three days. Russell himself does not think it sound to adopt

this attitude towards reality. It amounts, he says, to the elimi-
nation of Satan. True, H.E. can be held to have eliminated
Satan from his world. But he did not eliminate him by attack.
He did not call upon Satan to get behind him. He did not even
turn his back on Satan. He eliminated him by advocating his
restoration. He puts it this way in Volume I of *Impressions
and Comments:*

Stanley Hall has lately pointed out how much we have lost by
eliminating the Devil from our theology. He is the inseparable
companion of God, and when faith in the Devil grows dim
God fades away. Not only has the Devil been the Guardian of
innocent pleasure, of the theatre, of dancing, of sports, Hall
observes, but he preserved the virility of God. Ought we not
to rehabilitate and reinstall the Devil?

There is much psychological truth in this contention, even for
those who are not concerned, with Stanley Hall, for the main-
tenance of orthodox Christian theology. By eliminating one of
the Great Persons from our theology we not only emasculate,
we dissolve it. We cannot with impunity pick and choose what
we will dispense with and what we will preserve in our traditional
myths. . . .

In any case it must be said that mere grandeur, creativeness,
the apotheosis of virtue and benevolence, fail to constitute an
adequate theological symbol for the complex human animal. Man
needs to deify not only his moments of moral subjection and
rectitude, but his moments of orgy and revolt. He has attained
the height of civilization, not along the one line only, but
along both lines, and we cannot even be sure that the virtue line
is the most important. Even the Puritan Milton ("a true poet and
of the Devil's party without knowing it," as Blake said) made
Satan the hero of his theological epic, while the austere Carducci
addressed a famous ode to Satan as the creator of human civilization. And if you suspect that European culture may be only an
eccentric aberration, then let us wander to the other side of the
world, and we find, for instance, that the great Hawaiian goddess
Kapo had a double life—now an angel of grace and beauty, now
a demon of darkness and lust. Every profound vision of the
world must recognize these two equally essential aspects of Na-

ture and of Man; every vital religion must embody both aspects in superb and ennobling symbols. A religion can no more afford to degrade its Devil than to degrade its God.[1]

This was H.E.'s way of saying that morality is an art, that it is the *mores* of this moment and this place, while immorality so often turns out to be the *mores* of another time and another place. He did not desire to put more stress on the one than the other. "When we place ourselves at the high biological standpoint we see the vital necessity of each. It is necessary to place the stress on both." And again, "One may ask oneself whether it is not a pressing need of our time to see to it that these two great and seemingly opposed impulses are maintained in harmonious balance." That is really the main point of his long chapter on "The Art of Morals" in *The Dance of Life*, and the reason why it has been claimed that H.E. brought about Blake's *Marriage of Heaven and Hell*. Perhaps he expresses his view most clearly thus:

The more one knows of the real lives of people the more one perceives how large a part of them is lived in the sphere of Immorality and how vitally important that part is. It is not the part shown to the world, the mechanism of its activities remains hidden. Yet those activities are so intimate and so potent that in a large proportion of cases it is in their sphere that we must seek the true motive force of the man or woman, who may be a most excellent person, one who lays, indeed, emphatically and honestly, the greatest stress on the value of the impulses of Morality. "The passions are the winds which fill the sails of the vessel," said the hermit to Zadig, and Spinoza had already said the same thing in other words. The passions are by their nature Immoralities. To Morality is left the impulses which guide the rudder, of little value when no winds blow.[2]

The opposite to taking morality as an art is to take hard and fast rules, to hand ourselves over to some Great Moral-

[1] *Impressions and Comments.*
[2] *Ibid.*

ist. How many people really believe in doing this? It is notable how quickly moralists go out of fashion. Thus Kant was regarded as a very great moralist. Who now cares what he had to say under that head? "The art of morals was to him a set of maxims, cold, rigid, precise. A sympathetic biographer has said of him that the maxims were the man. They are sometimes fine maxims. But as guides, as motives to practical action in the world? The maxims of the valetudinarian professor at Königsberg scarcely seem that to us today." [1] There is a story told about Kant which I think is extremely relevant. He was very fond of sweetmeats. He made arrangements with his friend, Motherby, to have them specially imported for him, and on a certain day he was eagerly expecting a vessel with French fruits which he had ordered. The vessel was delayed by storm, the crew becoming short of provisions, ate the dried fruit. Kant furiously declared that they ought rather to have starved than to have touched it. Motherby showed some slight surprise at this irritation and asked him if he were in earnest. Kant insisted that he was, and though afterwards he said he was sorry, it is understood that it was in accordance with Kantian morality that the sailors should have starved. H.E. claims that it is not impertinent to refer to a philosopher's personality in relation to this subject. "In the investigation of the solar spectrum personality may count for little; in the investigation of moral laws it counts for much. For personality is the very stuff of morals. The moral maxims of an elderly professor in a provincial university town have their interest. But so have those of Casanova. And the moral maxims of a Goethe may possibly have more interest than either. There is the rigid categorical imperative of Kant; and there is also that other dictum, less rigid but more reminiscent of Greece, which some well-inspired person has put into the mouth of Walt Whitman: 'Whatever tastes sweet to the most perfect person, that is finally right.' " [2]

It may be agreed that this view is worth putting forward.

[1] *The Dance of Life.*
[2] *Ibid.*

In any case it can never make much headway, for we are all
absolutely riddled with negative moralizing. For every one
man in the world capable of a thorough experience of beauty
or religion, a thousand will moralize without a moment's
hesitation to consider. Yet there is a very easily spoken word
always in use—*tolerance*. We all think we have it. It means—
appreciation of diversity. We think we possess this appreciation: yet most of us are little superior to that small terrier,
once noted by H.E., with its critical, disdainful gaze as it
stood to watch a great goose pass by.

It is easy to accept art as an art, and not to consider a
painter's portrait as an ultimate; but H.E., in "The Art of
Thinking" in *The Dance of Life*, makes the same plea against
accepting a philosopher's system as an ultimate, and suggests
rather that we take it as an affirmation, as a means by which
we may make our own affirmations. After all what is a man's
philosophy but the *grouping* of his thoughts and impressions?
We all do this, and to that extent we make our philosophy,
whether artistically feeble or splendid. At one time I made
very little allowance for the extent to which a man's grouping
is a personal thing, fruit of his whole psychology. Confronted
with exactly the same phenomena another powerful writer
may easily give us an opposite view. It is the same with historians. At one time I looked to historians for Truth just as I
did to philosophers. But their grouping is just as much a
matter of personal art. It now never occurs to me to accept as
ultimate any historian's pattern of Decline or Progress or
Cycles or whatever it may be: I read him for his parade. It is
a liberating attitude; at least I find it so, and have knocked off
quite a few chains thereby.

H.E. did not write any masterpieces. His masterpiece is his
total *oeuvre*, the tree. Like a tree it grew steadily, branching
and leafing out in every direction almost simultaneously,
offering an unexampled range of phenomena from the physical to the spiritual; and if we study that totality we really do
attend at the marriage of heaven and hell. No doubt it would
have been easier for us and better for him if he had taken each

aspect in isolation—especially religion. The nearest he got to a masterpiece is *The Dance of Life*. But it lacks inevitability and drive: certain aspects could have been omitted or other aspects admitted. And when I say that it would have been easier for the public and better for his reputation if he had isolated his aspects more, I am thinking especially of "The Art of Religion" in *The Dance of Life*. A book devoted to this alone would have been very welcome, and it could then have stood out clearly for the world to take or to leave. That he did not do so may count against him, but it seems that he preferred his own natural method even if it meant that the main branch might be hidden by the foliage. I think he felt that it would be wrong to isolate religion; it is embedded in all his work, and this particular and vital chapter, "The Art of Religion," is embedded in the intensely loaded, perhaps overloaded and over-pregnant *Dance of Life*. It is at the centre and core of the book—as it was also his own core and centre —easy to see and to grasp if we take the trouble, but not emphasized, for he evidently wished to integrate it without fuss into his vision of life as a dance, a profound conception piercing to the very heart not only of life but of the universe itself based as it is on the dance of the electrons—for all physicists would agree that what follows from their Periodic Table is, quite strictly, a dance, the rule of number and of rhythm and of measure and of order, of the controlling influence of form and the subordination of the parts to the whole.

In "The Art of Religion" he states the Religious Question. I do not know where else to look for so satisfactory a statement. I took it yesterday to the Chesil Bank and tested it against the three things you get there—sea, sky, and stones. It stood up extremely well. The reader will know that by religion he did not mean theology—which is talk, conceptions. He meant religious *experience*. This is best called Mysticism, however much the term has been misapplied and abused by countless writers for countless years. It is an experience of enlightenment at a higher plane of consciousness, felt as harmony between the self and the not-self. Having the experience they can do without theology—though unfortunately they have often promoted theology. Ruling out those who, because they have not had any such experience on however humble a level, wish to take the view that the experience is bogus (which is not much more sensible than saying that a man who has been nourished by a good meal has not really had one at all), we may take Religion as a reality. Is there any conflict between it and Science? Is there opposition and hostility here? This question has so often been debated and has exercised bad thinkers so much that it has come to be thought a real question to be solved—or, better still, to be discussed forever. But it does not need to be solved. It does not come up. On the one hand we have an emotional response to the world and on the other the organization of an intellectual relationship to the world by means of which we get some degree of power over it. Why or how can opposition between these two different things arise? We have here two natural, fundamental impulses appearing spontaneously all over the world, and in early days were often embodied in the same individual—even in modern times, notably in H.E. himself. "The course of human evolution involves a division of labour, a specialization of science and of mysticism along special lines and in separate individuals. But a fundamental antagonism of the two, it becomes evident, is not to be thought of; it is unthinkable, even absurd." [1] What is not unthinkable or absurd is opposition between science and theology. Theology is not an experience but a set of beliefs and assertions which are thought to be true, and which may or may not be true. It is on the same plane as science, though, unlike the scientist, the theologian does not wish to modify or change his beliefs. Thus it would be strange indeed if there were no conflict between the theologian, the churchman, and science. But there is no greater hostility between the churchman and the scientist than between the churchman and the mystic. Indeed, the mystic is the greater enemy of the theologian, for while the

[1] *The Dance of Life.*

scientist only questions the beliefs, the mystic undercuts the whole edifice by unconcern; he does not concern himself, for example, with the-world-to-come, having no experience of it though ready to take it in his stride if necessary; nor concern himself about, say, Jesus walking on the water, since whether he did or didn't is of no religious consequence, though it may quite well be true, and may have been performed by others as well, just as not a few men, with no special pretensions, have even walked on air. The churchman is obliged to live under the perpetual pretense that science does not really undermine the essentials of his position and that the mystic is really only a nice man who, while not attaching himself to creeds, believes that "all religions are equally true." The harsh fact is that the mystic is much more likely to say that all theologies are equally false.

H.E. does not put the matter as offensively as this, but it is what he says in effect; and after having shown in a wonderful way "the real harmony between Mysticism and Science," he winds up by insisting that "all arguments are meaningless until we gain personal experience. One must win one's own place in the spiritual world, painfully and alone. There is no other way of salvation. The Promised Land always lies on the other side of a wilderness." [1] Is that a hard saying? I think not. It is only an exclusive saying. Those who need religion will have it. The many who do not need it will not miss it any more than they miss, say, a response to poetry. They need something perhaps. They can have ethics. And indeed, everywhere around us we see people happily imagining that ethics is the same thing as religion.

A further observation is called for. If the mystic does not stand on the same ground as the holder of creeds, neither does he stand on the same barren ground as those who call themselves agnostics or rationalists or atheists or freethinkers —the last often thinking so freely that it scarcely resembles

---

[1] The Dance of Life. I have gone no farther into this since I dealt with it in Section 5, devoted to H.E.'s experience, which he again speaks of in the chapter on "The Art of Religion."

thought. Thus the mystic has no horror of rituals and church services. For these things also belong to Life and to Nature. This was certainly the feeling of Havelock Ellis.

As the gracious spectacle of the Mass is unrolled before me, I think, as I have often thought before, how much they lose who cannot taste the joy of religion or grasp the significance of its symbolism. They have no faith in gods or immortal souls or supernatural Heavens and Hells, they severely tell us. But what have these things, what have any figments of the intellect, to do with religion? Fling them all aside as austerely as you like, or as gaily, and you have not touched the core of religion. For that is from within, the welling up of obscure intimations of reality into the free grace of Vision. The Mass is a part of Nature. To him who sees, to him who knows, that all ritual is the attempt to symbolize and grasp the divine facts of life, and that all the painted shows of the world on the screen of eternity are of like quality and meaning, the Mass is as real as the sunrise, and both alike may bring Joy and Peace to the heart.[1]

Again, his approach to the Funeral Service is the same.

The Funeral Service of the Church of England, when it becomes poignant with personal memory, is surely an impressive rite. As a religious statement it may cease to evoke our faith. But as an affirmation of the boundless Pride and Humility of Man it remains superb. When the priest walks before the coffin as it is borne towards the choir, and scatters at intervals those brave and extravagant Sentences, we are at once brought face to face with the bared and naked forms of Life and Death. For the rhythmic recurrence of that Bravery and that Extravagance only heightens the pungency of the interspersed elemental utterances in the rite, those pathetically simple gestures which impart to it Beauty and Significance, "We brought nothing into the world and it is certain that we can take nothing out. . . . Earth to earth, ashes to ashes, dust to dust." After all, it is hard to see how the solemnity of this final moment when Life touches Death, and a man at last vanishes from the earth's surface, could better be

[1] *Impressions and Comments.*

brought home in its central essence than by the splendid audacity of a rite which calls down the supreme human fictions to bear their testimony at the graveside to all their Creator's Humility and all his Pride.[1]

It must also be noted that neither does the mystic seek to undermine the significance of Jesus. He may open a new significance for all who are unable to embrace the Christian conception while respecting those for whom Jesus Christ is a mystical experience—though not in the least respecting the "unorthodox Christian," the modern Mr. Facing-Both-Ways. In one of his Impressions, H.E. speaks about how difficult and indeed impossible it is for us now to discern the features of the real Jesus, and how "around that concealed human person it is really the Imagination of Man which has built up the lovely crystal figure we see," an innumerable company of men each throwing into it his highest aspiration.

It was the peculiar virtue of the personality of Jesus that all these inspirations and insights could adhere to it and drew together into a congruous whole. At the same time a reversed process was evidently in movement. All the facts of the hero's life, actual or alleged, and all his sayings, real or apocryphal, were sifted and filtered through the human imagination, so purged that not a single trivial, ignoble, or even ordinary crude unpleasing statement has come down to us. At once by putting in and by taking out, with an art like that of the painter and the sculptor in one, under some rare combination of favouring conditions, the human imagination, out of the deepest impulses of the human heart, has unconsciously wrought this figure of Jesus, purified of dross and all gold, tragic in its sublimity and tremulously tender in its loving-kindness. So that now when I open and turn over with reverent joy the leaves of the Gospels, I feel that here is enshrined the highest achievement of Man the Artist, a creation to which nothing can be added, from which nothing can be taken away.[2]

[1] *Ibid.*
[2] *Ibid.*, p. 176.

He goes further. Even if it were supposed that Jesus never existed, we would still have the wonderful fact that he was invented. Even if we do not know whether the figure of Jesus is partly due to the imagination of man or wholly due to it, we could still say—"In either case how inspiring! The world is no longer presented to us as the little stage on to which suddenly rushes the bungling Playwright Himself in a wild and hopeless effort to mend the fiasco of His own actors. The universe expands and we see the soul of man rise to its own supreme rights, no longer the plaything of Gods, but itself the august creator of Gods." [1]

Havelock Ellis was a highly original person—aboriginal I have called him. But not original in his fundamental conceptions. We should not look for that in a great thinker. Originalities on the periphery, yes, but derivativeness must play a big part. H.E. was very derivative. That is to say he responded to certain imperishably valuable conceptions and made them his own. Thus, at the close of *The Dance of Life*, he preaches the development of our capacity to see the World as a Spectacle as the only way by which we may overcome the world. He shows how it was elaborately advanced by Jules de Gaultier and by Plotinus before him, and by others. Speaking of Plotinus's placing of Contemplation on the highest possible pedestal, beside religion and morals and as above art or comprehending art, H.E. writes—"It served to stamp forever, on the minds of all sensitive to that stamp who came after, the definite realization of the sublimest, the most nearly divine, of human aptitudes. Every great spirit has furnished the measure of his greatness by the more or less completeness in which at the ultimate outpost of his vision over the world he has attained to that active contemplation of life as a spectacle which Shakespeare finally embodied in the figure of Prospero." [2]

[1] *Ibid.*, p. 73.
[2] *The Dance of Life.*

Few are likely to quarrel with the idea that to be able to see the World as a Spectacle is of great consequence. For we know that it is the ultimate *raison d'être* of art, and even when we go to a poor film we are exercising that faculty and taking the sting out of tragedy and violence by seeing them as a spectacle; and when we exercise it in the highest mode it is indeed nearly a divine aptitude, we become as gods, with all the splendid callousness of gods. That is why art for art's sake is our salvation.

The mother who seeks to soothe her crying child preaches him no sermon, she holds up some bright object and it fixes his attention. So it is the artist acts: he makes us see. He brings the world before us, not on the plane of covetousness and fears and commandments, but on the plane of representation; the world becomes a spectacle. Instead of imitating those philosophers who with analyses and syntheses worry over the goal of life, and the justification of the world, and the meaning of the strange and painful phenomenon called Existence, the artist takes up some fragment of that existence, transfigures it, shows it: There! And therewith the spectator is filled with enthusiastic joy, and the transcendent Adventure of Existence is justified. Every great artist, a Dante or a Shakespeare, a Dostoevsky or a Proust, thus furnishes the metaphysical justification of existence by the beauty of the vision he presents of the cruelty and the horror of existence. All the pain and madness, even the ugliness and the commonplace of the world, he converts into shining jewels. By revealing the spectacular character of reality he restores the serenity of its innocence. We see the face of the world as of a lovely woman shining through tears.[1]

It is possible that this approach will have a strong appeal for many who yet, ignorant of their own elasticity, may feel doubtful and puzzled. "How can I take this view and yet battle against evil, meeting scorn with scorn and hate with hate?" They feel that they may be constrained in action. I think they are mistaken. We are more subtly built. We can see

[1] *The Dance of Life.*

and feel more than one thing at the same time. We strive amidst the dust of earth, and live within the noise and rumour of the field!—certainly, but even so, and even then, we can raise ourselves above the scene, and while in its very centre say with Melville—"Amid the tornadoed Atlantic of my being, do I myself still for ever centrally disport in mute calm; and while ponderous planets of unwaning woe revolve round me, deep down and deep inland there I still bathe me in eternal wildness of joy."

I think it can be said of the great spirits who with mighty words have struck away our chains, that though they have overcome the world they have not surrendered to delusion nor accepted imbecility. Consider these sentences from H.E.:

They are covered with honour. Men treat them with respect, women fall in love with them, ribbons and medals are pinned on their coats, nations are ready to starve to provide them with life-long pensions, they are encouraged—as we see this day—to form associations to demand for themselves all the best-paid posts in life and the dismissal of all others, women especially, now in employment.

And who are these heroes? They are the men, to whatever nation belonging, who were willing to be driven like sheep at the bidding of military imperialists in order to blast the world, who flung aside that personal responsibility which might be the divine prerogative of their species, cheerfully becoming machines to slaughter, loot, rape, and crush into nervous impotence every living thing within their reach, who have by their presence killed the sweetness and fruitfulness of every spot of earth they have swarmed over, and therein destroyed every achievement of human skill that could be destroyed, who have come near to undoing all the effortful attainments of graciousness and civility the ages had slowly wrought, who have made all life, so far as their hands could touch it, on the side they fought for as much as on the side they fought against, something fouler than Dante ever fabled of Hell—these are the creatures, slaves of slaves, mere clay in the hands of phrasemongers, who are the Heroes of Man.

O Man, sublime in dreams, pitiful in real life, august in the

creation of ideals, lower than an idiot in the face of the real
world, O pitiful Man, leave the world alone to be lived in by
those who know how to live; be content to dream.

But there is no one left to apostrophize Man nowadays. It
would be too rhetorical, it would not suit the mealy-mouthed
good breeding of our time. Like Agag we must go delicately,
and meekly be hewn in pieces.[1]

H.E. never courted popularity. He made no concessions
to the mob. Here he hits at the common man and much harder
than the popular Prophet ever dares to strike. For the *reality*
is that the common man knows perfectly well that he can
"strike," and have people at his mercy, and easily succeed in
getting higher wages when he chooses, but will *en masse*
goose-step in obedience to the phrasing of a fanatic, though if
he "struck," the same fanatic would be reduced to nothing, an
empty O.

That piece I have quoted was written in no mood of serene
contemplation. So be it! I have exaggerated in saying that it
is easy to see the world truly and to see it whole. H.E. acknowledged that it involves the harmonization of two dis-
cordant attitudes, and if only one is taken the man remains
only half a human being. "If he is only able to enjoy the absurdity of the world as a Spectacle, or if he is merely occupied
in solemnly striving to mould and cement it by Reason, he is,
in either case, a good half-man, but only a half-man." The
question is how to be at the same time both. "I have always
been preoccupied with this problem," he said. For only the
rarest great spirits have achieved it: Rabelais, Goethe, possibly
Shakespeare had he lived longer. To be the serene spectator
of the Absurdity of the world, to be at the same time the
strenuous worker in the Rationalization of the world—that
is the function of the complete Man. But it remains a very
difficult task, the supreme task in the Art of Living."

[1] *Impressions & Comments.*

26

HAVELOCK ELLIS did not employ, or rather, was not employed by the comic muse. Yet very often one reads him with amusement, in the strict sense of musing with a slight smile, at his novelty or his audacity or his irony or his cunning or his surprising twist. In "The Art of Thinking" he has a section on Vaihinger's *Die Philosophie des Als Ob*, subsequently translated and now famous as *The Philosophy of As If*—how we advance through means of fictions. The fiction of Force is a useful one, though we should bear in mind that it is only a tautological term, a reduplication of the fact that in reality we have only a succession and co-relation of existences, the "force" being something that we imagine. "It is one of the most famous, and also, it must be added, one of the most fatal of fantasies," says H.E. "For when we talk of, for instance, a life-force and its *élan*, or whatever other dainty term we like to apply to it, we are not only summarily mingling together many separate phenomena, but we are running the risk that our conception may be taken for something that really exists." I think we would have to look far for a more searching or a more teasing sentence. The element which separates literature from the perishable article is the element of *surprise*. It is that which makes us smile; and there is more in a smile than a laugh. Far from being a vegetarian, H.E. held that the practice was inconsistent with a high position of Man in the animal and spiritual world, and that no being could attain physical and spiritual success who was not able to eat all things eatable. "Those human people who wish to lay down arbitrary taboos on eating and drinking for the benefit of other people are always fair game. And have in some countries been eaten." [1] H.E. liked to be clear, but he also favoured irony which has been defined in its fundamental meaning as "pleasure in mystifying." That is one of the secrets of its appeal. "The saviours of mankind, with what at first sight seems an unkindly delight, have emphasized the fact that salvation belongs to the few. Yet not only is religion a sacred mystery, but love also, and art." [2] Or again—"An advocate of Anti-vivisection brings an action for libel against an advocate of Vivisection. It matters little which will win. (The action was brought on All Fools Day.) The interesting point is that each represents a great—or, if you prefer, a little—truth. But if each recognized the other's truth he would be paralyzed in proclaiming his own truth. There would be general stagnation. The world is carried on by insuring that those who carry it on shall be blinded in one or the other eye. We may call it the method of one-sided blinkers." And he adds—"It is an excellent device of the Ironist." [3]

I have myself derived most amusement from his cool remarks running flatly counter to the agreed and accepted thing. Thus, on Wordsworth: "The English genius is essentially romantic; all our poets of the first rank, with the single exception of Wordsworth, are on the romantic side. Wordsworth, whenever he is great as an artist, has the easy self-control, the clear outline and sane simplicity of classic art" [4] or on Karl Marx—"A student seated in the Library of the British Museum, consumed by enthusiastic zeal on behalf of the proletariat, and altogether remote from the actual economic facts of the developing proletarian situation" [5] or on

---

[1] *Impressions & Comments.*
[2] *From Marlowe to Shaw.*
[3] *Impressions & Comments.*
[4] *From Marlowe to Shaw.*
[5] *My Confessional.*

Carlyle—"The popular judgment is hopelessly wrong. We can never understand Carlyle until we get rid of the 'great prophet' notion. Carlyle is not a 'great moral teacher' but, in the high sense, a great *comedian*. His books are wonderful comedies," and again later, "the pathetic little figure with the face of a lost child, who wrote in a padded room and turned the rough muscular and reproductive activity of his fathers into more than half a century of eloquent chatter concerning Work and Silence." [1] And on Ruskin—"Ruskin was what Spinoza has been called, a God-intoxicated man; he had a gift of divine rhapsody, which reached at times to inspiration. But it is not enough to be God-intoxicated, for into him whose mind is disorderly and ignorant and ill-disciplined the gods pour their wine in vain." [2] I have quoted these remarks not only because of their non-dullness and as containing that element of surprise as precious as uranium, but because I take the liberty of agreeing with them heartily. Ruskin, spoilt by his parents, by a far too early success, by easy circumstances, and by the knowledge that whatever he wrote would be instantly accepted by publishers, printed, and praised, failed to discipline his work to a really shameful extent. Carlyle *was* above all things a comedian, a *funny man;* and it is that which makes his marvellous *French Revolution* an imperishable work. And while I am far more of a Wordsworthian than H.E. was ever likely to have been, and can take from him gladly the romantic rhapsodies, it is true that he is best when short and classic, as for example, "Glen Almain" in which certainly we find "The depth, and not the tumult, of the soul."

It is when the big men in the entertainment business come up for a view by H.E. that our amusement enters the field of entertainment itself. No one disputes the genius of Wells and Shaw in their department of story or play—and they had nothing to complain about in terms of wide recognition. Having the ear of the public they were prepared to preach salvation. But I think it may be said without offence that

[1] *The Dance of Life.*
[2] *Ibid.*

while they had many wise and brilliant things to say, fundamentally they were not much more profound than you or I.
This cannot be said of H.E. His was the genius of Comprehension—a rare and extraordinary thing. It was this which
caused Dean Inge to declare that H.E. was the only educated
man in the world. Thus it is truly amusing when Wells or
Shaw come up for inspection. They are met with extreme
urbanity and with something bordering upon severity. They
are given marks and placed quietly in a highly respectable
category, that of Prophet, shown to be a not quite first-class
place. You see, he is dealing with their thought and learning,
not their stories. Wells's *Mankind in the Making* comes before
him. He is at first very polite about the book and welcomes
the good intentions of the author. He adds, "To survey life
and to reorganize it, on so broad and sweeping a scale as
Wells attempts, necessarily brings him into a great many
fields which have been appropriated by specialists. Wells quite
realizes the dangers he thus runs, but it can by no means be
said that he has altogether escaped them. In this way he sometimes seems to be led into unnecessary confusions and con-
tradictions." He then advances some criticisms of what Wells
has to say under the head of heredity, of criminology, of
anthropology, and of evolution. It might seem that in the end
not very much was left upright. Under the last head, Evolution, Wells had expressed his belief as a self-evident prop-
osition that "man will rise to be overman." H.E. comments,
"While such a belief is certainly an aid to an inspiring gospel
of life, it can by no means be admitted that it is self-evident.
On the contrary, from an evolutionary point of view, there
is not the slightest reason to suppose that man will ever
rise to be overman." [1] Still, it will be better to take this in relation to Shaw whose *Man and Superman* came up for review.

He points out how Shaw had flung away many illusions
only to entrench himself in one remaining illusion—the Superman. "It is a vision that, from the time of Isaiah and earlier,
has always floated before the prophet's eyes and has always

[1] *Views and Reviews*, Vol. I.

proved irresistibly attractive to him: the supreme future man, the Messiah who will build up a new Earth, and whose path it is our business to make straight. There has never been a prophet who was not inflamed by that vision." He goes on to say:

Let us be cautious, however, how we use the word illusion here. Shaw will have it that love—and a fortiori the virtues ascribed to human institutions—are illusions, while the "Superman" is a piece of solid reality. When the doctrine is so stated, it is necessary to point out that this verity will not resist critical analysis any better than the others, and that it is by no means difficult to flay the "Superman" even before he is born. It is enough to say in passing that, granting to Shaw that "Our only hope is in evolution," the line of evolution has never been straight; in the natural course of things the successor of man would spring from a form lower than man; but as we have checked the lower forms of life at every point, we have effectually killed the "Superman." If he were to dig again into that Nietzschean mine whence he extracted the "Superman" Shaw might find another doctrine very much to the present point, the doctrine, that is to say, of the justification of "illusions" in so far as they are vitally woven into the texture of life and have aided in upholding humanity on its Course. Love is such an "illusion," the most solid reality in all the world, and without love, hard indeed will be the struggle to "replace the man by the Superman." [1]

The great thing in writing a book or in writing anything, is not to be dull. Even so there are wrong ways of avoiding this. Mere word crashing won't do the job. I have often heard it claimed how much more "lively" was D. H. Lawrence's criticism of books and of life than, say, the criticism in the Times Literary Supplement. That is true. But it could equally well be said that the Editorial Leaders of the Daily Express are more lively than those in The Times. It does not follow that they are better, it may only mean that they are tawdry. Lawrence could do wonderful things. A good poem of his

[1] Ibid., Vol. I.

was far better than the best H.E. could do in his *Sonnets*, from which I have not quoted; and we may be sure that had *he* written with the material and on the theme of H.E.'s *Kinga Creek, an Australian Idyll* (his one attempt at fictional autobiography) it would have been many times more powerful and compelling than H.E.'s effort. Those were the things Lawrence could do. They were not the things H.E. could do, just as he could not write a travel book or a gay letter—but how absurd it is to list what a man can't do. Unfortunately Lawrence thought and others claimed for him that he had the equipment to preach and to criticize. I think they are mistaken. Though not always, he was often tawdry to a degree (to wit, his essay on Herman Melville, cheap short-paragraph journalism, plus quotations actually misquoted on every occasion with his own inferior sentences shoved in instead!). I therefore think that I may, and indeed should, quote here the one and only reference to him in print from the pen of Havelock Ellis. It will help to balance things up.

"The ideal of love, the ideal that it is better to give than to receive— . . . all the lot—all the whole beehive of ideals—has got the modern bee disease, and gone putrid, stinking." It is not strange to see statements of this kind; they look familiar and one may pass them calmly. But it is perhaps strange that a man who is so anxious to get to the heart of things as Mr. D. H. Lawrence should be so befooled by the clang of words as to set the statement solemnly down.

"It is better to give than to receive." That is an ancient Oriental saying that has come down to us on what used to be thought good authority, and, as a matter of fact, it is profoundly true. It is put into the Oriental form, but one needs little intelligence to discern that the Orientals loved to make statements thus profoundly true in the form of paradox. In our more psychologically analytic way of stating the same truth, to give is better than to receive simply because giving is the most massive and deeply satisfying way of receiving.

Yesterday evening I gave a beautiful peach to a dear woman who, it appears, likes peaches but never feels that she is entitled to bestow such a luxury upon herself. It happens that I am indifferent to peaches. Yet if I were not, her delight in that fruit tasted far more delicious to me than even my own could. It was better to give than to receive because in giving I received far more than I gave. I do not know whether in my place Mr. Lawrence would have turned away with a woebegone countenance muttering to himself: "Bang goes saxpence!" But if there is any meaning in his outburst that is clearly what he ought to do. The same relationship exists even in what some consider the most egoistic of all impulses, that of sex. Twenty-three centuries ago, when it is commonly said that what we call love between men and women had not yet been discovered, Aristophanes was able to write in his *Lysistrata* that "there is no pleasure for a man unless the woman shares it." Even in this egoistic matter it is not only better to give than to receive, but one receives nothing unless one gives. If that is true in the most fundamental of natural relationships it is hard to see how there can be any relationship in which it is not true.

It sometimes seems to me that there are certain great elementary test sayings which if a man cannot make his own he is an alien in the world and a rebel from Nature, fated to be a disconsolate outcast from life. Of these shibboleths which only the children of Heaven, that is to say the children of Nature can utter, one is certainly this; It is more blessed to give than to receive.[1]

[1] *Impressions & Comments.*

27

THOSE who get the ear of the public almost invariably become windbags. Their deadwood has to be cut out by future generations—and what a lot there is to cut out! H.E. was not a windbag, his stuff is nearly all live wood, even the *Little Essays in Love and Virtue* have only a deadly and misleading title. He would have been one, you may think, if he had had the ear of the public in a big way. Yet that would hardly have been in character or capacity. In any case he did catch that Ear at the last. He was invited to write on anything he liked for an American paper once a week. At first he declined, then tried his hand with much success, and incidentally made £30 a week, which for him was phenomenal. These articles later appeared as *My Confessional* and *Questions of Our Day*. People wrote to him from all over the world asking him questions of every kind. Thus no man knew better than he did what people were thinking about and puzzling over; he had his finger on the pulse of the world. Sooner or later he replied carefully to each of his correspondents. *My Confessional* and *Questions of Our Day* amount to his replies polished up—a hundred and seventy-one in all. He starts with the question and then answers it in his own peculiar manner which never quite became a mannerism. He never made smart, brilliant, snap replies, but they are often surprising enough. I came to the conclusion on reading these, to me, very delightful books, that he had become master of his medium. He appeared to know exactly what he had in his mind and could set it down with as little appearance of effort as is discerned in a Chinese drawing of a bridge, a lake, a mountain, and a cloud. It might be described as a brilliant absence of "brilliance." Certainly it is a lesson in non-verbosity. You could scarcely substitute a sentence for another without loss of character. "And by the way," asks a correspondent, "do you think that Man's faculties will ever become sharp enough for him to discover the riddle of the Universe? If you will answer briefly, it will make me very happy." He had approached the right man—who did briefly show him how there are two distinct ways by which we may tackle the "riddle of the universe." An Indian, an M.A. and professor in a college, asks a string of questions—"Are you a non-believer in every religion? What do you think of Lord Jesus Christ? Do you believe that there are men now of practical courage equal to Socrates, and pioneers of thought equal to Aristotle and Newton?" How on earth will he start his answer to this little-knowledge-is-a-dangerous-thing man? It is characteristic. "I do not know what my reader's reactions may be to such questions. Mine is one of sadness. Not because I am for the most part no better able than anyone else to answer them. It makes me sad that anyone should ask them, or even desire any answer save his own. If on such matters of faith and belief a man cannot form his own opinions and stick to them, in complete indifference to the opinions of other people, what is his opinion worth? What indeed is he himself worth?" A friend who is a physician and also a psychoanalyst writes to him after the death of his wife. "Seeing her immense agony has not reconciled me to any theory of pain. It seems to me that pain is nothing but the crude imperfection of this life on earth. It has to be borne, but seems to have no compensatory virtue." The reply is pure H.E.-ism. "I have offered no other consolation to my friend. But I am touched by this simple and natural utterance as coming from one of whose profession it is a chief part to find remedies for the pains alike of the body and the spirit. I am far from accepting his statement, but this is a matter which has a personal aspect, sometimes hard to reconcile, and at the moment my correspondent is too overcome by the personal aspect to be able so much as to see that there is an impersonal aspect." After which he shows that "on that aspect nothing seems clearer than the beneficent character of pain."

Sometimes he enjoyed putting things in the wrong phrasing for the democratic moment. He notes that the proletariat has disappeared. "Meanwhile, we keep alive the unemployed remnants of the great proletarian armies of old. We either put them on the dole or we exercise charity. For in one country they like to feel they have a legal right to a dinner, and in another country they like to regard it as a gracious gift. It comes to the same thing."

The Great Question about the machine in modern civilization comes up. "The realists and the idealists were both wrong. Both alike—though they never knew it and do not indeed always realize it today—were fighting against Nature." And just as elsewhere he speaks of eminent philosophers failing to ask the right question, he adds—"For, as so often happens, the whole question would have fallen to the ground if only those who worried over it had taken the trouble to ask themselves the question—What is a machine?" I find this manner pleasing, whether or not the matter is always sound. He could be caught napping like any other man—as for example swallowing the prophecies that the next war (the last war) would destroy civilization. But he is never silly or stupid—as geniuses often are. Indeed it might be held that he was not enough of a genius to be outrageously silly at times. But that would fail to take into account that his genius lay in not being stupid or silly.

Every considerable writer employs more than one style if he wishes to do more than one thing. This is very marked with H.E. His style is sometimes poetic, sometimes audacious and subtle to the point of bravado (as in the already quoted passage on Jesus and St. Paul in *Affirmations*), and sometimes deliberately penny-plain. He knew when *not* to make a literary assault. A good example of this is *The Nationalization of Health:* no literary frills, just the case and the facts stated in clear language with only an indication here and there of other powers. He felt that a book of that kind would be more effective that way—as proved the case. Whereas Shaw's Preface to *The Doctor's Dilemma*, in which many similar things were said, was so much of a literary assault that the manner and not the matter engaged the attention of the public—and the wrong public into the bargain. Sometimes H.E. could be quite colourless, never more so, by the way, than in his little scientific brochure on *The Colour Sense in Literature.* And, it must be added, he was sometimes colourless, even lifeless, when he ought not to have been—as in his piece on Edward Carpenter in a symposium about him. In a great deal of his writing he was not concerned with making a literary effect—and that must have been very restful for him. But he often went all out, especially in *Impressions and Comments*, striving to make each entry a rounded little masterpiece—though on account of the entirely thoughtless fashion, this is supposed to be the prerogative only of verse! It goes without saying that they vary in quality and some contain what might be called *soft spots* (even in the best pieces) which blemish the material, while also I have been astonished at the number of times he uses the words *gracious* and *radiant*. Evidently they came to him so naturally that he was unaware of how he was spoiling them, though it must be admitted that only his thorough readers would notice this, and they would overlook it. Still, it is strange that so careful a stylist should have fallen into so elementary an error.

It is clear that, starting tentatively and experimentally with Volume I of the *Impressions*, he steadily gathered confidence and strength, so that in Volume III, while we do not get better things we do get his most audacious and aristocratic things. He was always the aristocrat in this mode. Élie Faure, speaking of him as "a beneficent devil in whose glory we participate," held the view that "because he really does love mankind he steadfastly remains the aristocrat to the point of seeming to dominate over man, even when he does not comprehend it, even when he does not know it, even when he is silent, even when he was always silent." [1] I'm not sure that I follow that, but it is rather delightful, and I have wished to include it. It is doubtful if H.E. loved mankind very much; he was certainly fond of *not* ingratiating himself with the mob or of giving a single glance at the box-office effect of not doing so. "For the Mob, huddled like sheep, around this Arena of Life, and with no vital instinct to play therein any part of their own, it is not for these to cast contumely. Let them be well content that for a brief moment it is theirs to gaze at the Spectacle of Divine Gaiety and then be thrust into outer Darkness." [2]

It will have been noted how often I have used in quotation the *Impressions*, for, as I have said, his total *oeuvre* is the masterpiece rather than any of the separate books, and I have needed the *Impressions* to illustrate certain points. Thus I have not been in a position always to quote what I happen to like best. Some readers may prefer it when his Impression and his Comment is direct and concrete, as when he speaks of the mosquito whose weightless feet alighting upon the skins of men have closed continents and destroyed civilizations— the piece ending with these words: "So that if we would see all of Nature gathered up at one point, in her loveliness, and her skill, and her deadliness, and her sex, where would you find a more exquisite symbol than the Mosquito," I would claim that he is most compelling when most oblique, the best example being "A Revelation" in Volume III, too long to quote, and I am unwilling to quote-and-cut for the same reason that I would not quote-and-cut a poem in verse. Obliqueness suited his angles best. One day just before Christmas, he passed by seven fat geese who greeted his approach with a chorus of loud cackling, and the thought occurred to him how much more pleasant it is to be faced with the cackling of geese

[1] *Havelock Ellis: An Appreciation.*
[2] *Impressions & Comments.*

than of men. After Christmas they had disappeared. "If only Pontius Pilate knew!" he adds. "How surprised that indolent sceptical Roman official might be could he know that the malefactor of whom he washed his hands and let go to the gallows would some day through that indifferent act become one with the Sun God, the Apollo-Dionysus of a new age, on whose Natal Altar millions of bloody sacrifices would all over the earth be offered up at the new birth of the Solar year by people who knew as little about it all as he knew, and cared no more! If only he knew!—And if we ourselves only knew the vast echoes of the things we do today!" Again, he sees some tulips, and by what I feel was a happy spontaneous chance, was able to make an oblique approach to a fundamental that was never far from his thoughts.

I was gazing at some tulips, the supreme image in our clime of gaiety in Nature, their globes of petals opening into chalices and painted with spires of scarlet and orange wondrously mingled with a careless freedom that never goes astray, brilliant cups of delight serenely poised on the firm shoulders of their stalks, incarnate images of flame under the species of Eternity.

And by some natural transition my thoughts turned to the incident a scholarly member of Parliament chanced to mention to me yesterday, of his old student days in Paris, when early one evening he chanced to meet a joyous band of students, one of whom triumphantly bore a naked girl on his shoulders. In those days the public smiled or shrugged its shoulders: "Youth will be youth." Today, in the Americanized Latin Quarter, the incident would merely serve to evoke the activities of the police.

Shall we, therefore, rail against the police, or the vulgar ideals of the mob whose minions they are? Rather let us look below the surface and admire the patient and infinite strategy of Nature. She is the same forever and forever, and can afford to be as patient as she is infinite, while she winds the springs of the mighty engine which always recoils on those who attempt to censor the staging of her Comedy or dim the radiance of the Earthly Spectacle.

And such is her subtlety that she even uses Man, her plaything, to accomplish her ends. Nothing can be more superbly natural than the tulip, and it was through the Brain of Man that Nature created the tulip.

I think this oblique approach serves him well here. He is enabled to insinuate into our minds without resistance the thought, the fact, that human nature is part of Nature and that it is idle to fight against Nature. Again, he felt that goodness and truth were not words to be used often or lightly, and that above all we should pause before we too easily talk of beauty and think of it as something which inheres in objects when it is really a rose on a bush covered with thorns, and that only "to the bravest and the skilfullest is it given to break through the briers of her palace and kiss at last her enchanted lips."[1] Near the end of the *Impressions* he does warily approach this Sign and packs his thought as tightly as Keats in his "Ode to a Grecian Urn," advancing one step further: "For my own part, I am quite content that I have always worshipped consciously at that shrine. Beauty, when the vision is purged to see through the outer vesture, is Truth, and when we have pierced to the deepest core of it is found to be Love. This is a goddess whom I have worshipped sometimes in the unlikeliest places, perhaps even where none else saw her, and she has given wine to my brain, and oil to my heart, and wings to my feet over the stoniest path."[2]

By this time the reader will have observed that I am in a fix. I am anxious to conclude. My time is up. Yet I go on quoting! True, I am finding it difficult to refrain, and it is true also that if I chose to substitute all that I have quoted for other things they would be just as arresting if not quite so relevant. Still, if my point is taken, I will now, with your permission, prepare to make an end.

It will doubtless have occurred to many that it is a pity that the literary works of Havelock Ellis are not widely known. It might even be said that they have fallen from sight, that

[1] *The Dance of Life.*
[2] *Impressions and Comments.*

they have been lost. It does not matter. When any good thing falls to the ground it is eventually picked up. These things have been lost. They will be found again. The reason is simple and sure. They have art. The property of art is endurance. It has a hard core. It is like a diamond. Empty a year's rubbish upon a gem: as the months pass the rain will soak, and the sun bleach, and the wind scatter, and the frost bite, and the air corrupt, until at last all that rubbish has perished from the earth. But the diamond is still there: it will glitter and shine for us as before it shone and it glittered. Empty a generation's literary rubbish upon a work of art, and though the pile will perish the art will remain. It will be found after many days, like that jewel the Queen dropped from the Castle walls, even after many centuries, to be treasured of men henceforth forever.

In 1882 H.E. made the following quiet remark in an article called "Two Worlds": "While, therefore, we recognize the service that Goethe and Walt Whitman have done towards bringing to us that great harmony, we know that the work is not done yet, and that we still look for the master-soul who, with hands loving and true, and insight broad and clear, shall, with fulness of knowledge, gather up for us into one expression the poetry and the prose of life. And that so the ideal world and the real world shall be reconciled. And can it be that we look in vain?" It has been claimed that he himself brought about that reconciliation. It may be so. If he could not do it, with his particular balance of power, we can scarcely hope that it ever will be done. I am free to say that he does it for me. Yet, even so, when I think of him it is not in such elaborate terms. Rather, I think of him as I do of the cock at dawn. It is a strange bird. It makes little appeal at first. It sings no song. It has no flight. Yet when it calls its message is like none other. It is the voice of hope and of assurance and of knowledge. In that lonely call there is a disdainful aristocratic isolation which chooses the earth's most silent moments to assert itself and trample down the phenomenal aspects of Nature in order to proclaim the triumph of some higher order. So it is with Havelock Ellis. His is not the music of the nightingale, nor does he rise with the lyric lark. We do not turn to him in the hour of triumph or gladness. Rather should we seek him when we are thrown into confusion or agonized with doubt, unable to face our present or believe in the future. Then we look to him who with such vigilance has kept watch for us, and say of him as he said of the cock: "At the hour when human vitality is at its lowest ebb, and despair nearest to hand, then it is that the watchman of the earth raises his voice and the cock crows: All is well with the world."

Works of Havelock Ellis

1890: *The New Spirit*
1890: *The Criminal*
1892: *The Nationalization of Health*
1894: *Man and Woman*
1898: *Affirmations*
1900: *The Nineteenth Century*
1904: *A Study of British Genius*
1908: *The Soul of Spain*
1911: *The World of Dreams*
1911: *The Problem of Race Degeneration*
1912: *The Task of Social Hygiene*
1914: *Impressions and Comments*, Vol. I
1916: *Essays in War Time*
1919: *The Philosophy of Conflict*
1921: *Impressions and Comments*, Vol. II
1922: *Kanga Creek*
1922: *Little Essays of Love and Virtue*
1923: *The Dance of Life*
1924: *Impressions and Comments*, Vol. III
1925: *Sonnets, with Folk-songs from the Spanish*
1931: *The Colour-Sense in Literature*
1931: *More Essays of Love and Virtue*
1932: *The Song of Songs* (Translation from Renan)
1932: *Views and Reviews*, Vols. I and II
1933: *Psychology of Sex* (Manual for Students)
1934: *My Confessional*
1936: *From Rousseau to Proust*
1936: *Questions of Our Day*
1937: *Poems* (edited by John Gawsworth)

1940: *My Life*
1945: *On Life and Sex* (combined and enlarged; Essays of Love and Virtue in one vol.)
1950: *The Genius of Europe* (edited by Françoise Delisle)
1950: *From Marlowe to Shaw* (edited by John Gawsworth)
1951: *Sex and Marriage* (edited by John Gawsworth)

This last short volume is probably not well known. My book, limited in scope both as a study and a biography, has not emphasized this field. Yet perhaps I may add here that *Sex and Marriage* might well prove helpful to many. Men and women wrote to Havelock Ellis about sex and marriage from every quarter. He often quotes representative cases. Reading such accounts reminds us of the endless subtlety of the problem. Thus a woman writes to say that she has got everything she hoped for, but is not happy. What is the cause? "I want something I have never got. What I mean is a sort of masculine virility, a sort of confidence in his own power to make a woman do his will, and even enjoying the resistance, though incapable of using physical force on a woman, while John's impulse is always to yield, and even if another lover appeared he would probably let the other fellow come in. Am I peculiar? Or do all women want lovers like that?" Perhaps we learn most—indirectly—from reading just that kind of letter.

The seven volumes in the *Studies in the Psychology of Sex* are:

I *The Evolution of Modesty, Sexual Periodicity, Auto-Erotism.*
II *Sexual Inversion.*
III *The Analysis of the Sexual Impulse, Love and Pain, The Sexual Impulse in Women.*
IV *Sexual Selection in Man. Touch. Smell. Hearing. Vision.*
V *Erotic Symbolsim, The Mechanism of Detumescence, The Psychic State in Pregnancy.*
VI *Sex in Relation to Society.*
VII *Eonism and other Supplementary Studies.*

INDEX